Guevara

Guevara

Frank Niess

translated by Nathaniel McBride

HAUS PUBLISHING • LONDON

Originally published under the title *Che Guevara* in the series Rowohlt Monographien
Copyright © 2003 by Rowohlt Taschenbuch Verlag GmbH, Reinbek bei Hamburg

This English translation first published in Great Britain in 2005 by Haus Publishing Limited
26 Cadogan Court
Draycott Avenue
London
SW3 3BX

Second edition published in 2007

English translation © Nathaniel McBride 2005

The moral right of the author has been asserted

A CIP catalogue record for this book is available from the British Library

ISBN 1-904341-99-3

Typeset by Falcon Oast Graphic Art limited
Printed in Dubai by Oriental Press

Cover image: Getty Images
Back cover: akg Images

Contents

Che the myth

There are few figures of the twentieth century who have become as famous as the Argentinian Ernesto Che Guevara. The French philosopher Jean-Paul Sartre called him 'the most perfect man of his time'[1]; others have seen in him the same qualities of many of the most outstanding figures of history. His forerunners would have to include such 'good men' as Francis of Assisi, Bartolomé de las Casas and Albert Schweitzer. Many in Latin America consider him one of the 'martyrs of the two Americas', ranking him among the freedom fighters Hidalgo, Morelos, Bolívar, San Martin, Zapata and Sandino. Indeed, the Cuban national poet Nicolas Guillen officially added him to this list when in his ode *'Che Comandante'* he placed

him in the 'pantheon of historic heroes of Latin America'.[2]

Europeans have been no less fulsome in their tributes, contributing to the Che myth by styling him a 'red Robin Hood', a 'Don Quixote of Communism', a 'new Garibaldi', a 'Marxist Saint-Just' or a 'Cid Campreador of the wretched of the earth'.[3] Other incarnations have included the 'first citizen of the Third World'[4], the 'man of the twentieth century'[5], 'one of the most outstanding ethical symbols in the history of civilization'[6] and, in a peculiarly metaphysical turn, the 'rebel Christ on the Cross'[7]. Guevara has entered history as 'San Ernesto' (de la Higuera) and as 'the Christ of Vallegrande'.[8] Indeed, it was not only the devout masses who hung photos of Che next to their crucifixes; some of their priests did so too. Nor are there many historical figures who have had so many songs and poems written about them – as many as 135[9] – not to mention plays, films, novels, collections of anecdotes and political cartoons. At the latest count, biographies about him run to several dozen, while academics have produced their own Che Guevara encyclopedia in addition to thousands of essays and monographs.[10] On the internet Che's presence is vast, with thousands of pages devoted to him.

Then there is the vast number of products and devotional articles bearing his image and name: beer bottles, cigarette boxes, bank notes, stamps, coins, towels, rings, bags, watches, ash trays, lighters, cups and, of course, T-shirts. Anyone who thought that Che's attraction would pale once his admirers among the generation of '68 had abandoned their idealism have found themselves proved wrong by the continuing tide of interest in Guevara.

The myth of the bearded rebel lives on. He has become a pop icon and a T-shirt hero of radical protest, an 'icon of revolutionary martyrdom'.[11] The marketing of this 'high priest of world revolution'[12] continues unabated, but so does the need to project onto him all number of unfulfilled longings and desires.

Why then has Che undergone this continual resurrection? The Uruguayan writer Eduardo Galeano has suggested, 'isn't it because Che said what he thought and did what he said? In a world where words and deeds so rarely correspond, isn't it this that makes him so extraordinary?'[13] There was in Guevara a unity of thought and practice that was fascinating and peculiar to him, and the aim of this book is to explain it.

Militant Upbringing

Childhood: the spectre of asthma

In his ancestors, Ernesto Che Guevara found exemplified many of the qualities that would later distinguish him: self-confidence, independence of spirit, daring and firmness of principle. Francisco Lynch y Arandia, one of his great-grandfathers on his father's side, of Irish and Spanish extraction, was forced to leave Argentina by the persecutions of the dictator Juan Manuel de Rosas (1829–1852). Another great-grandfather, Juan Antonio Guevara, had also fled the regime's repressions with his younger brother Jose Gabriel, and all three moved to California, where early in 1848 gold had been discovered near Sacramento. Though Francisco Lynch resisted the 'gold fever', building instead a prosperous business for himself in San Francisco, his brothers, like thousands of others, succumbed, and went to seek their fortune in the *'Placeres de California'*, the gold fields of the Californian hinterland. It proved a vain undertaking.

When de Rosas was overthrown in 1852 the men found themselves free to return home. The Guevara brothers set off at once, taking with them Concepción Castro Perralta, a farmer's daughter whom the older brother, Juan Antonio, had married in California, and their son Roberto. However, it was twenty years before Francisco Lynch returned to the Argentinian province of Mendoza with his wife and their daughter Ana. Ana fell in love with Roberto Guevara, and they married and had twelve children; among them was Ernesto, Che Guevara's father. Ernesto had little of his grandfathers' resolution and determination. Instead, he tended to coast through life, making a series of concessions in the hope of professional success.

He studied architecture in Buenos Aires after finishing school, but abandoned it in 1927 after marrying the twenty-year-old Celia de la Serna, a stylish and spirited woman from a 'good family' whose great-grandfather had been the Viceroy of Peru. 'Intelligent, capable and courageous', was how her husband Ernesto described her, adding that 'we got on very well together, since as well as husband and wife we were very good friends; and though we often argued over trivial matters, this probably had more to do with the fact that in our own ways we were very much alike.'[14]

Both of them could have been described as left wing intellectuals, with Celia taking stronger and more principled positions on matters than her husband. She was also more ready to take risks, and it was no accident that she came to be known as '*la rebelda*', 'the rebel'. Speaking of their common commitment to socialism, Ernesto Senior later quietly admitted that 'she quickly left me behind her'.[15]

Celia had grown up in a well-to-do family, but had lost her parents when still a child. Like her husband, she had had to share her inheritance with eleven brothers and sisters, leaving neither of them much in the way of material goods. The young couple took over a tea plantation they had inherited in the remote province of Misiones, where they planned to grow maté or 'green gold', the Argentinian national drink.

Ernesto had been deeply impressed by Misiones, a region in the north east of Argentina, bordered by the rivers Paran and Uruguay. 'Dense virgin forest – denser than you can imagine,' was how he would describe it, 'with trees over forty metres high and tangled undergrowth comprising a vast variety of plants; bushes, creepers and millions of ferns.'[16]

It was here that their son 'Ernestito' was born on 14 June 1928, and here that he spent the first two years of his life. Though it was clear to his father that his son was too young to be properly aware of this extraordinary environment, 'yet I am convinced,' he wrote, 'that all these experiences left a deep impression on his unconscious.'[17]

Che with his parents in Havana, 1959

The Guevaras' income from the maté plantation fell far short of what they needed to live on. So Ernesto and Celia decided to move to San Isidoro, on the banks of the Rio de la Plata, where Ernesto had a share in a shipyard. It was here, on 2 May 1930, that an event took place that was to horrify and terrify the family for years to come.

On that cold spring morning Celia, an excellent swimmer, went swimming with Ernestito, also known as Teté. When his father returned home at midday he found 'the child [...] trembling throughout his whole body'.[18] The two-year-old's condition worsened, and during the night he began to cough uncontrollably. A doctor was called and diagnosed asthmatic bronchitis. Ernestito's asthma became chronic.

It is one of the extraordinary facts of Che's life that this 'pathetic worm', this tiny asthmatic child, should have grown up to become an intrepid, ambitious and above all iron-willed revolutionary. Perhaps, though, it is precisely his illness that explains his remarkable career. Overcoming the fear of suffocation needed all his powers of resistance. Perhaps this was behind his fondness for sport – football, rugby, swimming; it certainly inspired his efforts, generally successful, not to let his chronic illness impinge on his life too far.

However, the ever present spectre of asthma remained a constant threat to family harmony. 'Like an evil curse', Ernestito's illness would turn his parents against each other. At every

Celia de la Serna with Ernestito

breathing attack his mother suffered terrible feelings of guilt, which his father reinforced with harsh reproaches, taking revenge for the many humiliations she had inflicted on him in their marriage.

The worst time for Ernestito came between the ages of four and six. He suffered asthma attacks at ever shorter intervals, and was unable to attend school regularly. His mother did her best to teach him at home. It was during this time that there developed 'the great love and friendship between them', as his father perhaps somewhat jealously noted. This is not to say that Celia neglected Ernestito's younger brothers and sisters; she treated them just as tenderly and lovingly. But for 'Teté' she always had a little more affection to hand.

Her son felt the same way about his mother. It is true he was very fond of his four siblings, especially his youngest brother Juan Martin, who was fifteen years his junior and whom he treated more like a son; but all his life he was closest to his mother. Later they became politically close as well. Wherever he was or whatever he was doing – as a young doctor, as a guerilla or as a politician – he always stayed in especially close contact with his mother. His letters, in which he kept her up to date with his travels, and which are largely concerned with politics, are a testimony to how much he must have loved and admired her.

He was the oldest son, and to a certain extent he took over responsibility for his younger brothers and sisters. Not because he wanted to be popular; he actually felt responsible. Perhaps because his parents' marriage was under strain. His father had many affairs [...] It wounded Ernesto that his father should have so little consideration for his mother's feelings. Ernesto was very close to his mother.

Dolores Moyano

First letter to his beloved Aunt Beatriz

Thirst for knowledge

Che's parents spared no pains in caring for their asthmatic son, and hoping that the climate in the capital would be better for Ernestito they moved to Buenos Aires. Their hopes were disappointed; their beloved son suffered there just as badly as he had in San Isidoro. Eventually they decided to cut all ties and to move to the healthier climate of north western Argentina. Their doctors advised them on Alta Gracia, a quiet provincial town not far from Córdoba, 600 metres above sea level at the foot of the Sierra Chica.

Following the birth of a second son, Roberto, the family settled there in 1933. First they stayed in a hotel, then moved to the 'Villa Nydia', a old, rambling house with a large garden, which became known among the so-called better citizens of the town as 'live as you please'.

Despite being in constant financial difficulties, Ernesto's parents did everything they could to live up to the libertarian spirit suggested by this name. Their house was open to everyone, regardless of social background and irrespective of whether they were rich or poor, and hordes of neighbourhood children would raucously avail themselves of it.

It was in Alta Gracia that Ernestito learnt how nature could be an 'important teacher'. In the surrounding sugar cane fields, and in the nearby woods and mountains, he grew to become an 'expert of the forest', as his father later proudly observed. This wasn't all, though; he also learned how to get his way among others. Whenever the children of Alta Gracia were planning some escapade, Ernestito was usually behind it. 'At the age of six he was already ordering all the neighbourhood children about'.[19]

However not everyone was so fond of him. Quite a few of his neighbours, schoolfellows and teachers found him insufferable; to them he seemed a rebellious, headstrong, troublesome, disrespectful and stubborn boy. To others he seemed quiet and introverted, to the point of being self-conscious and shy. Ernestito's illness forced him to be frequently

Ernesto with his sister Celia

absent from school, and he used this time to read everything he could get his hands on at home. He enthusiastically devoured adventure stories, novels and travelogues by Robert Louis Stevenson, Jules Verne, Alexandre Dumas or Jack London, to name but a few. His father Ernesto claimed that at twelve his son had read as much as the average eighteen year old.[20]

He also discovered Cervantes, Anatole France, Horacio Quiroga and the Chilean poet and Marxist Pablo Neruda, as well as the Spanish poets Antonio Machado y Ruiz and Frederico García Lorca. If his father's later statements are to be believed, then at the age of barely sixteen Ernestito had already read the Guevara household's entire collection of books; over 3,000 volumes on history, literature, poetry and especially politics.[21]

Although the Guevaras were in a manner of speaking aristocrats, Ernestito grew up in a decidedly egalitarian atmosphere, which both parents were equally careful to cultivate. He came to know people from every kind of social background, and this taught him the injustices of Argentinian society. Most of his friends came from the lower classes, and from them he learned the meaning of poverty, and what life was like for those working for starvation wages in mines, building sites and maté plantations without even the most basic social security. It gave him an insight into the unspeakable conditions that many of his playmates had to grow up in.

But the greatest influence on Ernesto during his childhood and early youth was the long shadow of the Spanish Civil War and the repercussions that it had for Argentina. During this time Celia's oldest sister Carmen and her two children were living with the Guevaras. Her husband, the Communist writer and journalist Cayetano 'Policho' Córdova Iturburo, had travelled to the front in Spain as war correspondent for the magazine *Critica*. He wrote regularly to Carmen, and his letters provided both precious evidence he was still alive and important information on the course of the war. In Alta Gracia it was therefore possible to build a fairly precise picture of events in Spain.

The Guevara family. From left to right: Ernesto jr., his mother Celia, his sister Celia, Roberto, Juan Martin, his father Ernesto and Ana Maria in Mar del Plata

Ernestito's parents supported the threatened republic unconditionally, passionately arguing its cause and gathering support where they could. Ernesto Senior established a local branch of the *Comite de Ayuda a la Republica*, a regional offshoot of the national solidarity network for the Spanish republic. He also made contact with the political refugees that were flooding into Argentina in increasing numbers. Among these were the doctor Juan Gonzalez Aguilar and the hero of the battle of Guadalajara (1937), General Jurado, who had defeated the Italian troops fighting for Franco on Spanish soil. Ernesto Junior listened spellbound as these eyewitnesses of the Spanish Civil War recounted their experiences. These, was his father noted, were formative experiences for him; 'Ernesto carefully cut all the reports out of the newspapers, and followed the troop movements on a large map of Spain that hung in his room, sticking little flags in the positions of the different fronts. I believe that his hatred of repressive dictatorships dates from this time.'[22]

The logical next step for young Ernesto was to go from listening to the adults talk politics to wanting to take part himself. At eleven he got his wish, when his father let him join the youth organisation of the local branch of '*Accion Argentina*' that he had himself founded in Alta Gracia. This organisation had set itself the task of fighting anti-semitic, racist and Fascist tendencies in Argentinian society.

It did so in a wide variety of ways. It organised rallies, collected money for the Allies, took action against Nazi attempts to infiltrate Argentina (notably by providing evidence that former crew members of the *Graf Spee*, the German battleship sunk in the Bay of Montevideo in 1940, had been engaged in espionage), and disseminated information on Allied successes in the war.[23] Whenever Ernesto Senior went scouring the mountains around Córdoba in search of traces of Nazi infiltration, Ernesto Junior would be with him.

In 1941 it came time for Ernestito to go on to secondary school; the nearest was in Córdoba. He had a long journey to school every day, with a round trip of about 70 kilometres; a terrible ordeal for a thirteen-year-old boy whose asthma showed no signs of improving.

The year in which Ernesto entered the *Colegio Nacional Dean Funes* was an eventful one. In July 1941 the German Wehrmacht invaded Russia; in December, Japanese airplanes bombed the United States' Pacific Fleet in Pearl Harbor. The Second World War was escalating, and the deadly confrontation between the Allies and the Axis Powers was coming to a head. It was a confrontation in which Argentina played a dubious role, not least because of its close economic ties with Nazi Germany. The country had resisted its neighbours' efforts to persuade it to side unambiguously with the United States. Indeed, far from declaring its support, it let itself be used by the Axis Powers as a base in the western hemisphere; one that was quite clearly to be used against the United States. It also became a focus for sinister political manoeuvres, with Nazis, Falangists and Fascists using it as a rendezvous for spies and a centre from which to disseminate propaganda.

President Juan Domingo Perón with his wife Evita

The main political event of Ernesto's youth was the seizure of power by the then unknown Juan Domingo Perón. An admirer of Mussolini and of Hitler, Perón was a leading member of the (to all appearances) neo-Fascist 'United Group of Officers' (GOU), had taken part in the coup against the ruling military faction, and had gone on to become first Minister for Labour, then Minister for War, and finally, in 1944, Vice President. More than anyone else in the new military regime, Perón inclined towards a progressive social policy. His populist programme included higher wages for the so-called 'little people' and more rights for trade unions. With the help of Eva Duarte, the woman who later became his wife, and who as a former singer and film actress enjoyed an almost mystical veneration as the 'Madonna of the Poor', his plan was to make the Labour Ministry a key instrument of his policy.

Clever, and with a shrewd populist style, he courted the descendants of Spanish and Italian workers who made up the majority in Argentina's largest trade union, the *'Confederacion General de Trabajadores'* (CGT). On becoming *'Presidenta'*, Evita took an active part in her husband's administration. Long queues of the *'descaminados'* or shirtless peasants and their desperately poor families would form outside her office, waiting reverently with requests for money, food, furniture or other objects of every-day need; and she, like a fairy godmother, would grant them.[24]

By helping to settle disputes over wages, import duties and employment rights in the workers' favour, Perón created a base of mass support for himself. Influenced by Catholic social teaching, he tended towards a regressive and undemocratic corporatism. However, the social peace and 'resolution of class conflicts' that he hoped to create with his wage and welfare policies would later serve more as a means of holding onto power.[25]

However popular Perón may have been among the working class, among the Left he was deeply loathed, particularly for his conservative Catholic nationalism. As far as they were concerned, he would always be a Fascist. However strongly he might insist that he wanted to emancipate the Argentinian working class, or free the republic from encirclement by foreign imperialist powers, the Left would never listen to him. The astonishing fact is that left wing intellectuals like Che's parents never countenanced supporting even a single element of '*justicialismo*', the 'middle way' he propagated between capitalism and communism.[26]

It is also extraordinary that during this time Ernesto was just as staunchly opposed to Perón as his parents, and did absolutely nothing about it. The fact was that in his early youth he made no effort to oppose the evils he would later denounce and fight; those of chronic electoral fraud, militarism, corruption, exploitation, capitalist economic order and 'Yankee imperialism'.

While his parents debated passionately over the dinner table, Ernesto would withdraw in silence to the corner of the room. He was equally laconic during political debates at school. At fifteen he did not join protests 'against the Fascist-inspired purges of the country's schools',[27] nor did he take part in any strikes against Perón's dictatorship.

During this time young Ernesto's behaviour showed a strange discrepancy between theoretical zeal and practical lethargy. While he closely followed international events, he seemed to be no longer interested in what was happening in Argentina, despite the political upheavals taking place. When at the end of 1943 Perón's chief General Pedro Ramírez outlawed political parties, enacted strict religious regulations and tightened press censorship, secondary school students and teachers went onto the streets to protest.

During the demonstration, one of Ernesto's best friends was arrested and jailed. Months went by without any charges being brought against him and his companions, and with no indication of when he might be released; eventually a solidarity committee was organised to demonstrate against this act of arbitrary power. Ernesto stayed away, giving as his reason, *What's the point of going out onto the street just to get beaten up by the police? I'm only joining when some-one puts a 'bufoso' (revolver) in my hand.*[28] Later, people tried to present him as a precocious socialist and a passionate young politician; on closer inspection, though, this proves to be a myth. He tried to correct this image himself, *{...} in my youth I wasn't the least interested in social issues, and in Argentina I never took part in any student demonstrations or political events.*[29] While his schoolfriends and fellow students demonstrated against Perón, he remained only an onlooker.

In 1943 his sister Celia entered the girls' grammar school in Córdoba; this gave the family a reason to move there and spare both children the punishing journey to school. Once again their parents were so short of money that they had to make do with extremely modest accommodation; a crumbling old house near a poor part of the city.

This doesn't seem to have particularly upset fifteen-year-old Ernesto. He continued to read voraciously and play sport as hard as he physically could – behaviour that was typical for him. He also seemed to have inherited his mother Celia's love of taking risks. In his memoirs, his long-suffering father recalls a number of occasions when his mother recklessly put her life at risk, including one when she almost drowned. He tells the story of how Ernesto decided one day to test his daring on a sort of railway bridge running twenty metres above a river; 'Ernesto would often balance over the precipice on the rails or swing hand over hand along the track from one side of the bridge to the other, while his friends turned away in horror. If there were girls were among the spectators he would become even more reckless and perform dare-devil balancing acts.'[30]

Becoming a doctor

The time came for Ernesto to decide what he was going to study at university. Given his talent for mathematics it might have seemed more likely that he'd choose to become an engineer, especially as he'd already worked for a road building company while still at school, an experience that had taught him a great deal about society as well as engineering. In a letter to his father at the age of seventeen he described the company as an unparalleled *heap of corruption*, before proudly recounting how *the foreman said I was the first worker he had known in twenty years who had refused any bribe, and one of only two or three who had not asked for one.*[31]

So his schoolfriends were surprised when, after graduating from high school in 1946, he decided to study medicine. The idea of becoming a famous doctor had great appeal for him; in particular an allergist who would someday develop an effective cure for asthma.

Another event confirmed him in his decision to study medicine; at the beginning of May his ninety-year-old grandmother Ana Isabel suffered a stroke. Ernesto not only respected his grandmother, he loved her deeply, and when the telegram arrived with news of how ill she was, he immediately resigned his job at the building company and got on the next train to Buenos Aires. His father recalled that 'Ernesto did not leave my mother's bed, and tried any way he could to relieve her suffering. All of us could see that she was gravely ill. Ernesto was in despair to find that his grandmother was no longer eating, and tried with extraordinary patience to feed her himself. He stayed with her until the end.'[32]

While at school and university Ernesto had developed an almost fanatical reverence for the truth, but he had also acquired a reputation for pig-headedness and for always having to have the last word. His friends found him full of contradictions. He was a notorious loner, but he could also be very sociable. His vast breadth of knowledge gave him a reputation for being a walking library, but he never played the arrogant intellectual. He was capable of being extraordinarily sensitive to those around him, and at the same time both wildly egocentric and appallingly harsh on many of his contemporaries.

The story of his first great love shows how he dealt with these contradictions. He was besotted with a girl called Maria Carmen Ferreyra, nicknamed 'Chichina'. The two had already known each other a long time, but a passionate romance suddenly developed between them after they met at a wedding in October 1950. At the first sight of Ernesto Chichina was 'utterly captivated',[33] and he was no less smitten by her. It is this that makes the ambiguous tone that he later adopted in a letter of 5 December 1951 all the more surprising. *I know how much I love you and how very much I love you, but I cannot sacrifice my inner freedom to you*, he admitted to her. *That would mean sacrificing myself, and to me I am, as I have already told you, the most important thing in the world.*[34]

An enemy of all convention, Che had been well brought up and was capable, when it suited him, of deploying the most beautiful manners; he was a man of iron will, strong character and deep human feelings; a man who simply was what he wanted to be: a fighter for justice, who hated to see others suffer and was destroyed opposing it [...] When you considered him closely, you knew why you admired him, and you knew that, whatever happened, you would always like him.

Arnol Rodriguez Camps

These lines spoke of an egotism that must have deeply shocked Chichina, but it did not yet lead to a separation between the two '*novios*' (fiancés). Clearly the attraction between these two very different people was still strong enough to withstand a breakup at this point. 'He fascinated me,' Chichina later admitted, 'he had a steady gaze, and a brave, defiant manner that showed he didn't give a damn what anyone thought of him.'[35]

Ernesto evidently enjoyed provoking Chichina's father, the millionaire Don Horacio Ferreyra, a representative of the feudal class responsible for the country's political repression and pervasive corruption. Even the clothes he wore to the Ferreyras' ostentatious villa seemed shocking to Chichina's parents and their guests from the local high society. To them Ernesto looked like a bum. He 'would appear in a shirt that he washed only once a week. He wore it every day, it was already quite grey, and he called it his "weekly shirt". Once when he couldn't find his belt he took the washing line [...] and wrapped it around his trousers.'[36]

But his contempt for bourgeois convention went far beyond how he dressed, and he affronted respectable society with his strange behaviour. Nevertheless people – with the exception of the fairly apoplectic Señor Ferreyra – tended to overlook many of these infringements of the social rules. Ernesto was self confident and good looking enough to get away with it, as well as being able to be utterly charming and personable; undoubtedly the most important thing at this stage.

His fiancée's affections, however, were not limitless. She couldn't understand why Ernesto's fascination for all things foreign and exotic – which would soon lead him on long journeys across South America – should increasingly come in the way of his feelings for her. His studies in distant Buenos Aires already only allowed him to visit her sporadically, and now even this was threatened by his plans for travel. The two found themselves growing apart.

New horizons

The old saying that travel broadens the mind was especially true for Ernesto Che Guevara. He had none of the wanderlust or curiosity of a young bourgeois intellectual; he never meant to gather impressions on the history and culture of his destinations with which to impress elegant society; on the contrary, it was 'hatred for civilization' that set him on his travels.

The people he met on his first journey across northern Argentina could rarely hide their incomprehension that *someone should be making such an uncomfortable journey for the sheer hell of it, for the pleasures of nature, of travelling across unknown regions, of seeking new horizons and meeting new people.*[37]

This first great journey was certainly uncomfortable. Guevara covered more than 4,500 kilometres, mostly by himself, and on a vehicle that was anything but sturdy or safe; a Micron, really more like a motorised bicycle than a motorcycle. Its *favourite trick was breaking down on steep slopes.* Ernesto frankly admitted that *the brakes on my bike didn't work very well, which meant that I had to be very careful going downhill.*[38]

He'd set off on from Buenos Aires on 1 January 1950, and was to find many steep hills along the journey; a journey he may have taken to escape arguments at home.

Much of what Ernesto recorded in the way of events, experiences and feelings during his tour of northern Argentina, a region known as the country's 'poorhouse', reveal a great deal

On a tour of discovery through Argentina with the Micron motorcycle, 1950

about his personality. For example, when he describes how having arrived one night in Rosario at the end of one leg of his journey, his *determination to ride on* overcame his leaden weariness, and he braved a heavy downpour with neither the raincoat nor the tarpaulin that his mother had carefully given him for his journey, but only a mordant sense of humour; or how, against all advice, he had set out for the famous Salinas Grandes in the middle of the Argentinian desert with only half a litre of water. *But the fine mixture of Irish and Galician blood that flows through my veins prevailed, and I cast this well-meant advice aside.*[39]

He relished the forms and colours of the landscape he crossed, meeting along the way itinerant workers, peasants, soldiers and other Argentinians from the lower classes. He also got to know several 'cultivated people', including the family of a senator who kindly took him in without knowing who he was. But without question the most moving incidents for him on this journey were the meetings and experiences that concerned his ambition to become a doctor. Principal among these was his visit to a leper colony where Alberto Granado, one of his best friends, was working.

Alberto Granado was also to accompany Ernesto on his next great journey, a *real journey* as he later put it.[40] Granado was six years older than Ernesto, and his rather cooler temperament and greater experience of the world made him the ideal travelling companion on their journey through western South America. They set off on 29 December 1951.

It was an October morning, Guevara later recalled, *I'd taken advantage of the national holiday on the 17th and gone to Córdoba. On the terrace of Alberto Granado's house we drank sweet maté and discussed the latest incidents in this 'wretched life' while tinkering with the Poderosa II.*[41]

The *Poderosa* or 'Mighty One' did not remotely live up to its name. It was a antiquated vehicle that threatened to give up the ghost and fall apart at any moment. *With its two huge saddlepacks and its luggage rack with all our things stowed on it, including the grill for the churrasco and the camp beds and tent, the motorcycle looked like a prehistoric monster*. This 'mighty' mode of transport also had a tendency to throw its driver and pillion off like a horse bucking its rider at a rodeo.

Throughout the journey, the '*Poderosa II*' would be constantly breaking down and needing technical improvisations to get it on the road again. Eventually, on 2 March 1952, mid-way along their journey, the two travellers were forced to abandon it in Santiago de Chile.

From then on they made their way by hitch-hiking or hiding in the backs of trucks, getting by by finding casual labour here and there. Often, though, they found themselves completely broke, and when that happened there was nothing for it but to *scrounge their way out of things*.[42] When talking of their busy days in Cuzco, Ernesto frankly admitted that *our life {...} never lost the quality of hard slog that it had had throughout the journey*.[43]

When the *reprobates*, as they liked to call themselves, couldn't find a barracks or a police station to spend the night in, they sometimes had to make do with somewhere genuinely uncomfortable – a garage, a lorry, a shed or a kitchen belonging to some friendly Chileans, Peruvians or Bolivians they'd got to know.

More often than not, they'd find an *animal hunger*[44] gnawing at their guts. At these moments they cast good manners aside. *With out stomachs rumbling we decided to abandon the last shred of shame we had left, and headed for the hospital*. There Che announced to a rather surprised doctor, *I'm a medical student, my friend is a biochemist; we're both Argentinians and we're hungry. We want to eat. Surprised by this kind of frontal attack, the doctor can think of nothing than to take us to the pub where he went for lunch and tell them to give us some food. We were ruthless*.[45]

The two young medics weren't only prey to their *empty stomachs*. Asthma, Che's chronic handicap, added to the difficulties of their journey, and wrecked many of their plans. *Asthma and mosquitoes clipped my wings somewhat, but virgin forests have such a fascination for spirits like ours that physical problems and all the forces nature could unleash only served to increase my desire*.[46]

Their journey first took the two motorcyclists to Miramar, on the Atlantic coast. At this popular seaside resort Che had to make a romantic interlude, as he later ironically put it; a final meeting with Chichina. Their journey then took them southwards, to Bahia Blanca, where they turned west. They reached San Carlos de Bariloche on 11 February and three days later crossed 'the imaginary but real line that separates Argentina from Chile'.[47] As they did so, they were expecting not to be strangers in a strange land beyond the border, but to find themselves in familiar Latin American surroundings where they would make new friends.

The two men arrived in Santiago de Chile on 1 March 1952 and, after a short stay, continued on to Valparaiso. Their hopes of visiting Easter Island were dashed when they learned that no ship was going there for months on end. Disappointed, they changed their plans and stowed away on board the *San Antonio*, bound for Antofagasta. Once they'd got over their seasickness, the captain ordered the bos'un to give them something to eat and some work to do. Ernesto was sentenced to cleaning out the *famous toilet,*[48] while Alberto was given potatoes to peel. They landed on 11 March, but didn't want to leave Chile without visiting the famous saltpetre and copper mines of Chiquicamata.[49]

When they finally left the country they had learned a good deal about its society. While still on their way to Santiago de Chile in the south, small tenant farmers in the countryside had spoken to them of the poverty and injustice they suffered. This gave the two travellers an opportunity to speak to their hosts 'cautiously of agrarian reform, and how the land ought to belong to those who work it'.[50]

After all he had heard about the people's everyday life, Ernesto came to the conclusion that *the Chileans' standard of living is lower than the Argentinians'*.[51] While the people in the south of Chile complained of low wages and lack of work, the workers in the copper, saltpetre, sulphur, gold and other mines of the north faced high prices and barbaric working conditions.

After visiting the mines Alberto and Ernesto both agreed that *the main thing Chile has to do is get its tiresome Yankee friend off its back, a Herculean task, at least for the time being, given the huge US investment and the ease with which it can bring economic pressure to bear whenever its interests are threatened.*[52]

Again and again, the two friends encountered a painful contrast between the beauty of the land and the misery of its people – first in Chile, but later also in Peru and Bolivia. What particularly shocked the two young Argentinians was the depressed state of the countries' native Indians; they seemed a 'shapeless mass of listless beings, dulled by coca and alcohol'.[53] Physically and mentally they were in no condition to resist the exploitation and glaring social injustice to which they were subject.

After visiting the colonies on Lake Titicaca, one of the main tourist destinations, and the Inca monuments of Machu Picchu, Cuzco and Lima, the two *iquitos* headed on into the Peruvian rainforest. From there their route went by motorboat up the Amazon to the leprosarium at San Pablo. Ernesto and Alberto had in the meantime put it about that they were 'two scientists visiting all the leper stations in the world'.[54] In the Chilean town of Temuco Che had already had a laugh over a news report in the paper announcing 'in the local news section, under quite a big headline' *two leprosy specialists from Argentina travel across South America*.[55] The cheek of claiming to be important figures in American leprosy research amused him no end. The diaries the two 'leprosy experts' do not relate whether they made important new discoveries in San Pablo, or whether the 'results of their research' made any contribution to the treatment of the disease.

Ernesto Guevara travelled home via Miami, *setting foot on Argentinian soil again* in October 1952. He felt he was returning a different person. *This aimless roaming across our vast continent has changed me more than I thought,*[56] was how he put it.

No sooner had he returned than he was thinking of the next big journey. First, however, he had to put things on some kind of firm footing, and this meant finishing his studies as quickly as possible. Given that he had to earn his own keep at the same time, this was no easy task. 'He worked as a medical orderly on board merchant navy freighters and tankers; he had a trainee job in the city's health department working in the allergy clinic [...] of Dr Pisani; for a while he made and sold insecticide, and he had a job at the Buenos Aires welfare office.'[57]

He set to work with the determination that characterised everything he did in life, giving himself a deadline: he would finish university by May 1953. He had all of seven months until then, during which time he had to pass fifteen examinations. He let nothing and no one distract him or put him off, not even the political unrest then prevailing in Argentina. Most nights he would retire to his father's study where could work undisturbed; or he would go over to his Aunt Beatriz's home to revise, where she would serve him maté all night long. Che Guevara could go without a great number of things; he could, for example, go for days without food; but studying, travelling, reading, working or fighting without maté was beyond him, and had been since childhood.[58]

He finished his last exam on 11 April 1953. Ernesto Guevara Lynch was in his office when his son telephoned him to say, *This is Doctor Ernesto Guevara de la Serna*, pronouncing the word *doctor* with audible pride.

If his parents now hoped that their son would realise his dream of 'becoming a famous research scientist [...], making a pioneering discovery that would benefit humanity',[60] the newly qualified doctor had to tell them he had a better idea. Nothing in fact came of the brilliant career as a scientist and asthma researcher that the family had envisaged for him. After he had finished his exams, Ernesto bluntly declared that would be leaving again on this travels, this time with his old friend Carlos Ferrer.[61]

'On a cold, grey day in July 1953 the whole family gathered at General Belgrano station to see the two travellers off. [...] When the guard blew his whistle we kissed, embraced, shouted goodbyes and waved handkerchiefs. I ran beside the train for a few metres and heard him call [...] "Today there sets out a soldier of America!"'[62] At the time it this seemed a strange thing to say; only later would it become clear that with these words Che had announced his life's ambition.

He and his friend Ferrer had boarded the train for the north and Bolivia, and from the high plateaux they slowly wound their way down to La Paz, the highest capital in the world, and not a city known for its cosmopolitanism nor for a particularly Latin American *joie de vivre*. The thin air, the cold and above all the chronic depression evident in the withdrawn faces of its Indian population made every action an effort of will, including political action.

Bolivian Indians

This made the Bolivian revolution of 1952, which had returned to its indigenous people something of what had been taken from them by their Spanish conquerors, all the more remarkable. Centuries before, the Aymaras had cultivated the altiplano, practicing what was virtually a form of primitive Communism that eschewed all individual property rights. At that time had existed the institution of '*Ayllú*', a central element of Quechua and Inca culture, which ensured that all descendants of the same ancestors held land in common. By now, though, all this was only a distant folk memory. Simón Bolívar had returned land to Indians who had been robbed and enslaved; but the authorities had taken it away from them again in the second half of the nineteenth century. It was not until the revolution of 9 April 1952, which brought with it land reform and nationalisation of the tin mines, that peasants and workers were freed – at least for a while and to a certain extent – from the bonds of serfdom in which the big landowners and tin barons had effectively held them for centuries.

The Nationalist-Revolutionary Movement (*Movimento Nacionalista Revolucionario* or MNR) took power under Victor Paz Estenssoro. Workers' militias forced the hated oligarchy and the no less despised army from government, while in the countryside landless peasants occupied the 'haciendas', the vast estates belonging to the big landowners.[63]

These events had spread unrest and commotion, upsetting the even and stoic temper of highland life. 'People danced in the streets'[64] – a quite unheard of phenomenon. Ernesto, however, didn't let himself get carried away by the euphoria that accompanied the reforms. The Argentinians he got to know in La Paz noticed his scepticism, among them the 'sugar baron' Isaías Nougués, the richest of his compatriots in the city. It was at his house that Ernesto met Ricardo Rojo,[65] a fellow countryman and a lawyer by profession who had gone into exile after serving a long term in a Buenos Aires jail. At first Rojo barely noticed the 25-year-old doctor of medicine; 'The first time I met Guevara he made no great impression on me. He spoke little, preferring to listen to others; but every now and then he would smile disarmingly before coming out with a devastating remark.'[66]

Many people must have been irritated by Ernesto's disparaging assessment of the Bolivian revolution. *We should be fighting the causes instead of contenting ourselves with solving the effects*, he wrote. *This revolution will fail if it doesn't manage to jolt the Indians out of their intellectual isolation {...}, speak to their deepest hopes and give them back their humanity.*[67]

To people directly involved in bringing about social change in Bolivia, this stern warning must have seemed presumptuous if not downright arrogant; but it wasn't without foundation. Always observant of what was going on around him, Ernesto had been shocked by an incident he'd witnessed in the lobby of the Ministry of Agriculture. While waiting there to interview its head of department, Nuflo Chávez, he noticed a group of Indians who had come to collect the title deeds promised them by the land reform. Before they were allowed in, however, they were sprayed with insecticide to disinfect them. This gave Ernesto the opportunity to observe sarcastically that *the MNR was making the revolution with DDT*.[68]

After they had decided to continue their journey, Ernesto wrote to his father on 22 July, *It's a shame we can't stay longer, since the country is interesting and going through an extremely turbulent period right now*.[69] Other destinations were calling, though.[70] Except for Rojo, who went directly on to Ecuador, the young Argentinians took a brief detour into the past, visiting the impressive Inca remains at Machu Picchu and the ruins of Sacsahuamán; Ernesto, a brilliant amateur archeologist, was captivated by the ancient Peruvian treasures.

Ernesto, Ferrer and Rojo met up with each other again in Ecuador.

Guayaquil on the Rio Guayas is a dilapidated and unbearably humid town standing in the middle of a swamp desert, itself a breeding ground for yellow fever and parasitical infections. Travellers arriving there soon find themselves longing for the coolness of the altiplano. It was here that the three of them had to wait before continuing their journey – and it was here that Ernesto suddenly changed his travelling plans.

His friend Alberto Granado was working in a leper colony in Venezuela, and he had solemnly promised that he would visit him there once his exams were over. It wasn't like Ernesto to break his word, but Rojo knew how to be persuasive. 'Why do you want to go to Venezuela? That country's only good for earning dollars' [...] 'Guatemala's the place to be now,' he added, 'there's a revolution going on there, and an important one; we should see it.'[71]

A left wing revolution in the United States' 'backyard' and one that Washington had opposed more strongly than any other in Central or South America – such a prospect was too great a challenge for Ernesto Guevara to turn down, especially given the prospects it opened up for the rest of Latin America. He changed course from Venezuela to Guatemala.

What is more, he wanted to leave as soon as possible. The steamy heat of Guayaquil left him short of breath, and one asthma attack followed another. At the shabby hostel where he was staying it was virtually impossible to get a full night's sleep. And his finances were in just as bad a shape as his health. Ernesto wrote to his mother on 22 October that he was going to go to Guatemala. He admitted quite openly that he had sold the suit she had given him before leaving for a few pesos. *The pearls of your dreams*, he wrote, *met a heroic end at the hands of a tinker, as did everything else in my kit that I could sell.*[72]

On 31 October 1953, Ernesto boarded the *Guayos* bound for Panama. He had no plans to spend much time in a country that had effectively been created by Washington in 1903 to protect its

The former sergeant Fulgencio Batista, who seized power in 1952 in a military coup, in front of a relief map of Cuba

interests in the Canal. From Panama he travelled overland to Golfito in Costa Rica, a little port on the Pacific coast. There he had his first encounter with the all-powerful United Fruit Company, the huge North American conglomerate. *I've had the chance*, he wrote to his Aunt Beatriz on 10 December 1953, to travel through land belonging to the United Fruit Company, *and discover again the terrible nature of this capitalist monster.*[73]

In the Costa Rican capital of San Jose, Ernesto happened to meet two Cubans; Calixto García and Severino Rossel. A few months earlier they and about a hundred others had tried to storm the Moncada barracks in Santiago de Cuba. The barracks were the second largest on the island, and their aim had been to seize the army's weapons to use them to overthrow the country's dictator Fulgencio Batista.[74] Militarily the daring operation had been a disaster. Most of the rebels had been killed the same day, 26 July 1953, with two notable exceptions – Raúl and Fidel Castro. Politically, however, the storming of the Moncada proved to have lit a beacon that signalled the beginning of a long struggle.[75]

Political apprenticeship

Baptism of fire in Guatemala

By the time he arrived there on New Year's Day 1953, Ernesto had learnt from the two exiles some sense of the political importance of what was happening in Guatemala, a country then known as 'the greatest testing ground of Latin American revolution'. He would become both a witness and participant in the events of this desperately poor country; and these experiences would influence the rest of his life.

Events had started to gather pace in Guatemala in 1944, when an uprising of students, workers, peasants and several members of the armed forces had overthrown the bloody regime of General Jorge Ubico y Castañeda. A period of reform followed, bringing its citizens as yet undreamt of political, social and economic progress. One of the soldiers who had helped introduce the reforms was Jacobo Arbenz Guzmán, a landowner and a captain in the army. In 1950 the Guatemalans elected him president with an impressive two-thirds majority.

Contrary to expectations, Arbenz did not set himself up as the typical *caudillo*, but continued instituting reforms that benefited the weakest in society. One of his first acts was to raise the minimum wage to a dollar eight cents a day, a measure designed to help the poorest of the poor achieve a tolerable standard of living. Eventually, with his Decree No. 900 of 17 June 1952, he initiated a land reform.[76] There was not a hint of radicalism to this thoroughly moderate reform, and nothing about it that could remotely be described as socialist.

Nevertheless it unleashed a storm of indignation, principally in relation the land belonging to the United Fruit Company (UFC) that Arbenz had allowed to be expropriated. Known as 'el pulpo', the company was effectively a state within a state, its interests deeply connected to Washington politics. Secretary of State John Foster Dulles had been a lawyer for the company for many years. His brother and head of the CIA Allen Dulles had been president of the UFC and the man behind its expansion overseas; while the then Undersecretary for Inter-American Affairs, John Moors Cabot, was a major shareholder.[77]

A skillfully orchestrated press campaign spread scare stories of a Soviet takeover of power, creating the impression that Arbenz's government was composed entirely of Communists. Faced with a possible foreign invasion, the regime began arming itself by buying weapons from Europe; North American politicians immediately seized this opportunity to declare the USA's 'national security' under threat. In Washington's Latin American policy this had long been considered a justification for posting warships off the supposed enemy's coast and sending the Marines in against it. In Guatemala the task of restoring 'peace and order' to the banana republic was delegated to a mercenary army under the command of Colonel Castillo Armas, supported by the United States air force. On 27 June Arbenz was forced to resign. His successor to the presidency was none other than Castillo Armas; and one of his first acts in office was to repeal the land reform.

Ernesto learnt a great deal from watching these events unfold, in which Armas played the part of his 'negative teacher'.[78] He had experienced counter-revolution at first hand and received an object lesson in, among other things, the way big business and government work together. The other crucial lesson was the behaviour of Arbenz himself, who had handed victory to the enemy by his passivity and indecision.

With the mercenary invasion imminent, Guevara went to offer

his medical services to the Guatemalan health authorities. He got nowhere. The officials in the air-conditioned offices didn't know what to do with such an offer. Even after the US-backed 'Operation Success' had begun, Guevara was still vainly trying to get youth organisations, trade unions and peasants' cooperatives to arm themselves and oppose the invaders; but even this came to nothing. He later admitted in an interview with the Argentinian Jorge Ricardo Masetti how disappointed he had been in the Guatemalans' reluctance to fight; *{...} when the North American invasion landed, I tried to organise a group of young men like myself to confront the adventurers of United Fruit. In Guatemala it was necessary to fight and almost nobody fought.*[79]

In a letter home he said that *In Guatemala I grew up. I became the kind of person who makes a true revolutionary.*[80]

It was also in Guatemala that he became 'Che', a word meaning workmate or friend. In Cono Sur, in southern South America and Argentina, it is a common mode of friendly greeting, roughly translatable as 'alright mate?' As Guevara used the Guarani word 'Che' in almost every sentence, his Cuban friends got used to calling him 'El Che Argentino' and then simply 'Che', which sounded friendlier and than the more formal 'Ernesto'.[81]

And we can be certain that 'we can more or less precisely say when and where he discovered Marxism. It was in Guatemala in 1954; in part influenced by his wife Hilda Gadea Acosta, who belonged to the left wing of the Peruvian APRA, and in part by the "Alliance of Democratic Youth", a mass organisation linked to the PGT (Guatemalan Workers' Party), which he had joined. In Hilda's library and in the library of the Alliance he got a thorough grounding in the writings of Marx and Lenin.'[82]

In Hilda Gadea Che had found someone who was both like-minded and his intellectual equal. At the political and social gatherings in Guatemala many women had gazed longingly at him without managing to get his attention; but the Peruvian woman won him over. She was utterly committed to her political mission, as Che himself would soon be. In her work as a leading activist in the APRA youth movement, she had angered the dictator General Manuel A. Odría and had subsequently had to leave the country. In Guatemala she found both a safe place of refuge and a job that suited her revolutionary energy, working in an organisation that promoted the country's agriculture and its still very modest industrial development.

Hilda Gadea lived in the same boarding house as Che and his companion Rojo, a modest but comfortable dwelling where the guests inevitably got to know each other. Had he been interested only in getting her into bed, the young Argentinian would almost certainly have disdainfully ignored her, for she did not remotely correspond to the prevailing ideal of beauty. Short and stocky, with high cheekbones, slightly slanting eyes, olive-coloured skin and straight black hair, Hilda's Indian ancestry was obvious; her physical appearance was the extreme opposite of Chichina's. Che, much to his discredit, once said of her, *Too bad she's so ugly*.[84]

Despite this she was to play – next to his mother, or rather as a mother substitute – a central role in his life. She was a committed revolutionary with a lot more political experience than Ernesto, and who knew in Guatemala City, that capital of Latin American exiles, a great many others active in left wing politics. Among the people she introduced him to was Nico Lopez, a veteran of the storming of the Moncada; it was he who persuaded Che to support Castro's cause.

There was also the fact that, unlike Che, she had a job and was earning money; she was therefore able to help him out of a lot of financial difficulties, most notably when the rent came due. She even tried to help Che out of his troublesome financial dependency by going job-hunting for him, though without success. The money Che earned through casual labour, working among other things as a book and newspaper vendor, was enough to keep him from starving; but it wasn't enough to live on.

Hilda not only helped look after Guevara's health, particularly during his terrible asthma attacks, she also had a great influence on his intellectual development. As a kind of respected authority on Marxism she introduced him to a whole canon of related literature, above all to Mao.[85] It was from Hilda that he received his first book on the Chinese revolution, and he returned the favour by giving her works by Sartre, Freud, Adler and C.G. Jung. When Che wasn't talking politics with his friends or working on *The Role of the Doctor in Latin America*, the book he was writing, he buried himself in the works of Marx, Engels and Lenin, as well as Latin American writers like the Peruvian José Carlos Mariátegui.

When, after a brief stay in the Argentinian embassy, he was finally forced to leave the country where he'd received his 'political baptism of fire', he did so having learnt one lesson above all others; 'Guatemala,' said Hilda after his death, 'convinced him once and for all of the need for taking up armed struggle against imperialism, and of going onto the offensive.'[86]

'Working class life' in Mexican exile

By the time Guevara arrived in Mexico City on 21 September 1954, his ideological equipment was impressive. Castro later modestly admitted that 'I think that, ideologically at least, Che Guevara's development as a revolutionary was more advanced than mine when I met him. As a theoretician he was more fully formed; as a revolutionary he had progressed further.'[87]

Like the others who had sought asylum in the Argentinian embassy, Guevara had been offered a flight home on a military aircraft. He had declined, asking instead to be allowed safe passage into Mexico, where Hilda, his new 'novia', soon followed him. A year later, in September 1955, when events in Argentina were gathering pace after the fall of Perón, Ricardo Rojo again tried to

Habla Fidel. Fidel speaks. Castro has long known how to enchant Cubans with his distinctive style of public speaking

persuade Che to return home when he stopped off in Mexico on his way back to Buenos Aires. *No, I'm not going. What for?* Guevara had replied. *Something extraordinarily important's happening here; what the Cubans are doing is gathering support every day.* Even the prospect of a genuine revolution in his own country couldn't lure him away. To indicate the fate he predicted for any regime coming to power from such a revolution, 'he drew his finger across his throat as if cutting it with a razor blade'.[88]

It is hardly surprising that when the moment of decision came he should have chosen to stay in Mexico. Not only had the country experienced a revolution, it had also proved its independence from the Gringos in the late 1930s under President Lázaro Cárdenas; partly by instituting a land reform and partly by nationalising its oil fields.

Its capital Mexico City was famous for being a centre of cosmopolitanism. Exiles and victims of persecution from all over the world and from every kind of regime found refuge in the city's urbane and permissive atmosphere, among them writers, musicians and artists.

At the same time, public services in this enormous city were too overstretched to provide any help for individual refugees arriving there. On 30 September, nine days after his arrival, Guevara wrote to his Aunt Beatriz that *Mexico, the city or rather the country of the mordidas has received me with all the indifference of a placid wild animal: it neither licked my hand nor bared its teeth.*[89]

Everyone had to find their own niche where they would be able to get by in the mega-city, and Che was no exception. He scraped a living working as an allergist and a researcher in the Hospital General and in the children's hospital of Mexico City, as a nightwatchman, as a reporter for the Argentinian news agency, Agencia Latina, and as a street photographer.[90]

Che with his wife Hilda and daughter Hildita, 1956

Che had arrived in Mexico accompanied by Julio Roberto Cáceres Valle, a Guatemalan Communist known as 'el patojo', in Guatemalan a nickname for 'shorty' and in Spanish for 'bow legs'. The two of them worked as a team. *'El Patojo' had absolutely no money and I had only a couple of pesos; I bought a camera and together we set about clandestinely photographing visitors in parks. Our partner was a Mexican with a small laboratory where we developed the films. We got to know the whole of Mexico City from walking from one end to the other and trying to sell our terrible photos.*[91]

Che obviously hadn't been reluctant to leave Hilda, and while he was on his way to Mexico she had planned to return to Peru. Despite this he did assure her, albeit with a certain cold formality, that they would meet again in Mexico, and there was even talk of getting married. But he made clear what he really planned to do when he wrote on the day of his departure that *I think I'm using the fact that she can't yet leave to finally end things between us.*[92]

Hilda, however, did follow him to Mexico and resumed the role of breadwinner in his *working class life*, as he woefully described it. By working in an office she was able to earn enough for them to rent a small flat; on 15 February 1955 a daughter, Hilda, was born to them, known as 'Hildita'.

The young Argentinian had felt Guatemala to be a sort of personal defeat, and had arrived in the political turmoil of Mexico City with high ambitions, determined to compensate for the traumatic experience of defeat. At first he was concerned simply with survival, but his political aspirations and revolutionary strength of purpose soon reasserted themselves. Given the size and nature of the exile community living in Mexico City in 1954, it was only a matter of time before he would meet other like-minded people, and it was probably in July or August of 1955 that Che got to know another convinced 'American' living in exile, Fidel Castro.

Guevara might reasonably have been asked what business he had becoming involved in the politics of other Latin American countries like Guatemala, Cuba and Bolivia. His answer would have been simple; he considered the 'latinos' a single 'family', who had to stand together in the struggle against the 'colossus of the north'. Like José Martí, Cuba's national hero, who had envisaged a distinct and independent United Latin America emerging from the subcontinent's patchwork of national states, Che dreamt of Latin American unification, of *'Nuestra America'*.[94]

His travels in South America had strengthened his sense of being a Latin American first and foremost and an Argentinian only second. The reverence he showed for Martí was a sincere expression of his own feelings, *He's more than just a Cuban; he's an American. He belongs to every one of our continent's 20 countries.*[95] But the independence and unity of Latin America had first to be won; and won, what is more, from the United States, whose hegemony over its self-declared 'backyard' had prevented the unification of the countries of the subcontinent since the days of James Monroe. For Che, the cause of Latin American unification – though not only this cause – was inseparable from an open 'antiyanquismo' or anti-north Americanism. In a heroic gesture, Che the Latin American patriot swore to give his life for the freedom of any Latin American country.

Che Guevara displays his admiration for José Martí, Cuba's national hero, who fought against Spanish colonial rule at the end of the nineteenth century and had farsightedly warned of exploitation and repression by the 'Colossus of the North', the United States

'No people of America is weak,' states the Second Havana Declaration of 1962, 'for each is part of a family of two hundred million brothers, all of them suffering the same misery and cherishing the same hopes, all of them facing the same enemy and dreaming of a better future [...].'[96]

Che hoped that these two hundred million would one day rise up and storm the bastions of the oppressors and exploiters. In his mind's eye he saw the entire people of America, spurred on by Cuba's example, arming itself for revolution, and he was optimistic enough to prophesise that *The Andes will become America's Sierra Maestra.* He has been described as 'the heroic Comandante of America's dawn'.[97] *Many of the people of America are ready for revolution*, he declared, adding that *The people of America know that the hour of liberation is near.*[98] In his *Message to the Argentinian People* of May 1962 he was already talking specifically of socialist revolution as the only effective solution for Argentina and the whole continent.[99]

José Martí was born in Havana on 28 January 1853. By the age of 16 he was already in trouble with the Spanish colonial authorities. After a serving a term of hard labour in a stone quarry, he was 'pardoned' and sent into exile in Spain. There followed years of study and travel in Mexico, Guatemala, Venezuela and New York, 'the belly of the beast', as he called the United States. His experiences there turned Martí, a poet, journalist and politician, into a passionate proponent of Cuban independence and Latin American unity, he became known as 'The apostle of a free America'. He was killed on 19 May 1895 fighting against Spain in the Second War of Independence. In Cuba he is revered as a national hero.

The first meeting with Fidel

I met him on one of those chilly Mexican nights, and I remember that our first discussion was about international politics. A few hours later that night, in the grey light of dawn, I had become one of the future members of the expedition.[100] That is, he became a potential member of the 'armed expedition to Cuba' that Castro and his comrades were planning; a second attempt to free Cuba from Batista's

Fidel Castro was born on 13 August 1926 in Biran in eastern Cuba, the son of a well-to-do farmer from Galicia. He decided to dedicate himself to politics while studying law at the University of Havana. On 26 July 1953 he and more than a hundred others led a failed attack on the Moncada barracks in Santiago de Cuba in an attempt to overthrow the dictator Fulgencio Batista. After spending several years in jail and then in Mexican exile, he led a war of liberation against Batista, who fled the victorious rebels on 1 January 1959. Since then Castro, known also as 'Comandante en jefe' and 'Máximo líder', has stood at the head of the Cuban state.

dictatorship following the ill-fated attack on the Moncada barracks of 1953.

It was the meeting of two revolutionary kindred spirits: Castro, the strategic head, the planner, who directed the painstaking preparations for the operation with exceptional organisational skill and extraordinary energy; and Guevara, the revolutionary romantic, the masked idealist, who brought such passion to the revolution's utopian ambitions that even by the expeditionary force's less abstract thinkers could grasp them. Che exultantly said of his relationship with Castro that *From the beginning Fidel and I were united by a feeling of romantic longing and adventure, and the conviction that it would be worth dying on a distant shore for such a fine ideal.*[101]

On 18 October 1967 in Havana's Revolution Square, Castro paid homage to 'the genius of the art of guerilla warfare' in these terms; 'Che was an incomparable soldier, with an incomparable talent for leadership. In the field he was a extraordinarily able man, extraordinarily courageous and extraordinarily militant. If he had any flaw as a guerilla it was this excessive militancy that was unique to him; that, and his utter disregard for danger.'[102] It was a description that implied criticism as well as praise.

The Cuban exiles had found in Guevara both an intrepid comrade and a doctor with experience of tropical climates; but they would also find they'd gained a brilliant thinker, a theoretician who, unlike Castro, knew from the beginning where he wanted to take Cuba after the revolution, namely towards Communism.

Most biographies accept the received wisdom that it was in Guatemala he 'discovered'[103] Marxism and became a Communist. This is true if by 'Communist' is meant an idealistic young man for whom capitalism, and in particular the 'American way of life' with its brutal domination of Latin America, had come to seem ever more hateful. But even after the bitter experience of counter-revolution in Guatemala, he remained for some time nothing more than a keenly interested political observer.

He was, however, an observer of world events who was progressing from a sporadic to a systematic reading of Marxist texts. Between 1954 and 1956 he concentrated on studying political economy, burying himself in Marx's *Capital*. *Until then*, he admitted in 1956, *I had more or less dedicated myself to medicine, and had studied St Karl {Marx} only in my spare time. This new phase in my life demands a change in priorities; St Karl comes first now, and everything else has to fit in around him.*[104]

Eventually he started describing himself as a Communist. In late June 1956, when the Mexican authorities had got wind of the young revolutionaries' preparations for a guerilla war in Cuba and their conspiracy against Batista seemed in danger of collapsing, Che was arrested and sent to prison. Under investigation he declared himself a supporter of Communism and armed revolutionary struggle, both in Cuba and throughout the whole of Latin America. Here he was already displaying the firmness of principle that would soon become legendary and so exasperate the Cubans. Years later Castro mildly rebuked Che for having been at the time so 'excessively honest'. The fact was of course that he had been furious when he learnt that Che had made this extremely foolish admission.

There were many other tests to be gone through before the rebels could make their crossing to Cuba. They had to acquire weapons for themselves, find a farm in the country where they could carry out target practice and go through guerrilla school under the tuition of a veteran of the Spanish Civil War, General Alberto Bayo. In addition they had to evade the Batista regime's attempts to foil their plans and prevent their return to Cuba.

The nimbus of the guerrilla
Comandante Che Guevara

By 25 November 1956 their preparations were ready. The 83 rebels boarded the yacht Castro had acquired for them in Tuxpán, a small port on the Gulf of Mexico. It was a leaky, ageing vessel whose name, *Granma* or 'grandmother', inspired little confidence in its sea-worthiness. The same night they slipped slowly out of the harbour with their engine muffled and their lights dimmed. The weather was bad, and as they entered the open sea it quickly became clear that the crossing was going to be an ordeal. Most of the *companeros* went down seasick, while the ship itself turned out to be hopelessly overladen. Having had to leave much of their equipment behind, the rebels now found themselves forced to throw a good deal of the remainder overboard; things that later would be desperately needed.

They landed at Niquero, on the south-western tip of Cuba, and though the crossing had been disastrous, what they would encounter there would be far worse. Supporters under the command of Frank Pais were supposed to launch a popular uprising that would divert the army from the *Granma's* landing. The plan failed when *Granma* had arrived several days late; then the uprisings only served only to alert Batista's army of its landing. Castro and his men were met with a hail of bullets. Starving, exhausted and demoralised, the survivors of the first bombardment were forced to seek shelter in dense mangrove thickets, where they recovered as best they could. Then to crown his misfortunes, Che was struck down by a long and particularly severe asthma attack.

On 5 December the army attacked again with an air bombardment at Alegría de Pío. Che was wounded and later recalled that he thought he was going to die. When he told one of his comrades that they would have to surrender, the latter snapped back, 'No one's surrendering here'; these harsh words came from Camilo Cienfuegos, who would go on to play a crucial role in the war of liberation, especially when it shifted from the Sierra Maestra to the plains.

Cut off from each other, and knowing nothing of each others' fate, for several weeks the rebel groups wandered through the mountains more or less aimlessly. The conditions they lived under were appalling, and it was

History will absolve me. Only death can free people from such misery. And indeed the state does all it can to help people towards an early death. In the countryside ninety per cent of the children are infected with parasites [...] Society is appalled when it hears of a single child being abducted or murdered, but it behaves with criminal indifference towards the mass murder of so many thousands of children, who are condemned to die in agony every year because the proper facilities for treating them are lacking.

Fidel Castro's defence speech
of 16 October 1953

all they could do just to survive; *We didn't have a single thing to eat all day, and water was strictly rationed by distributing it in the eyepiece of a set of binoculars so that everyone received the same amount. That night we resumed our march and got as far away as we could from place we'd spent one of the most terrifying days of the war. Plagued by hunger and thirst, painfully aware of our defeat and knowing that a very real danger was pursuing us, we felt like cornered rats.*[105]

Three urgent tasks now faced them; to recover from the attack, find their missing comrades, and finally to abandon the desperate defensive position into which they had been forced. The rebels would achieve all of these things in the weeks that followed.

Their first military engagement took place in the early hours of 17 January 1957, when the rebels mounted a successful attack on a small army barracks they'd spotted by the La Plata river. *It was the first battle the rebel army won; and this and the following encounter were the only ones in the whole campaign when we had more weapons than men {...} The peasants weren't ready to join the struggle, and links with support groups in the city were virtually nonexistent.*[106]

All this would change in the months that followed. At the same time living conditions, which had at first been so calamitous, gradually improved for the rebels. They no longer had to avoid lighting fires by day for fear of air attack, nor exhaust themselves by having to hack their way through undergrowth with a machete, nor spend the night soaking wet and without a change of clothes when it rained, nor find themselves so short of food that a meal of four sausages seemed a *marvellous feast*; above all, they lost the oppressive sense of being under siege. On 12 February 1957, the guerrillas who had survived the fiasco at Niquiero finally met up with each other again. The *United Revolutionary Army* now numbered all of eighteen men.

Though unwilling to join the conflict, the peasants found themselves being increasingly drawn into the guerrilla war whether they liked it or not. At the beginning at least, they found themselves caught between the two sides. On the one hand, the rebels made it ruthlessly clear what would happen to them if they betrayed their movements or plans to the regime; namely summary trial and execution. On the other, Batista's soldiers would torture and murder *campesinos* on the slightest suspicion that they were supporting the rebels' cause. *A wall of mutual mistrust towered between them {the peasants} and the guerrillas. {...} Mad with fury, the criminal dictatorship ordered the deportation of thousands of guajiro families from the Sierra Maestra and into the towns.*[107]

However, opinion gradually shifted in favour of the guerrillas. As the war progressed and the rebel army came to occupy whole swathes of country, it became clear to the peasants were better off allying themselves with the bearded rebels, regardless of whether they sympathised with them politically or not. Eventually the majority of them came to switch sides.

The people of the Sierra vegetate like untended wild plants, Guevara recalled, *and they quickly wear themselves out in unpaid drudgery. Seeing them at this back-breaking work, we realised very clearly that their lives needed to be fundamentally transformed. The idea of a land reform took distinct shape, and our solidarity with the people went from theory to practice as this became a matter of basic concern for us.*[108]

It would be going too far to say that real unity gradually developed between the guerrillas and the peasantry, but the rebels did manage to establish a relationship with the smallholders and farm labourers of the Sierra Maestra that secured them from attack in the rear. If ever there were any guerrillas who, in Mao's words, were able to move among the peasants like fish through water, it was the Cubans. The crucial thing in establishing this working relationship was the rebels' behaviour towards the peasants. Unlike the soldiers of the regime, they didn't go marauding across the country, robbing and murdering its inhabitants and relentlessly spreading terror; instead, they treated them as civilized human beings. They also paid for all the food and other kind of help that they needed from the *campesinos*, issuing IOUs when they had no cash.

But they did more than this. With very modest means at their disposal, the revolutionaries, and Che Guevara especially, set up a sort of rudimentary welfare system in the Sierra, which offered at least some relief to the peasants' vegetative existence and appreciably alleviated their poverty.

In the first *nomadic stage* of the liberation struggle Guevara had the job of doctor, looking after the sick and wounded. A new phase began for him in May 1957 when he became an active soldier, rising to become '*Comandante*', the highest rank in the rebels' military hierarchy. However, his new responsibility did not stop him pursuing his public welfare plans.

He held 'surgeries' for the local population in every area the rebels came through, and people would come to him with diseases such as rickets, parasitic infestation and vitamin deficiency. Though he often lacked the medicine to help his patients, it was something new to this desperately poor people for anyone to be taking any kind of interest at all in their plight, and his treatment had at least a psychologically beneficial effect for them.

The rebels set up medical posts, a small saddlery, a cigar factory, a smithy and an 'arms factory' of sorts, all of which the peasants were allowed to use. Long before the nationwide literacy campaign of 1961 they built rudimentary schools in the 'liberated territories'; another novelty that was taken by the local population as a sign of respect.

Reading at every opportunity. Guevara immerses himself in Goethe during a break in the fighting

The 'liberated territory' in which Batista's army no longer dared to venture was growing from month to month. By April 1957 there existed a clearly demarcated area that the enemy did everything it could to avoid. Armed with new weapons and with increased troop strength, the guerrillas launched their first daylight frontal attack on one of the army's fortified bases at El Ulvero on 28 May 1957. One of the bloodiest battles of the war, it was both militarily and psychologically a brilliant victory, and had enormous repercussions for the whole country. To the revolutionaries it seemed that they had finally cracked the secret of how to defeat the enemy, and their morale was greatly lifted.

Batista's troops withdrew from the coastal areas of the Sierra Maestra. *The operation at El Ulvero sealed the fate of all the enemy's small garrisons.*[109] Not long afterwards the guerrillas managed to surround the enemy for the first time and put him to flight. By the end of August 1957 Batista's army had withdrawn entirely from the Sierra Maestra.

The rebels' campaign had now transferred from a *nomadic* to a *settled stage*, and they proceeded to assert their control over *the liberated territory of Cuba* by setting up a system of justice. Though the army no longer set foot in this region, the guerrillas also weren't strong enough to make their presence felt everywhere or to set up a comprehensive system of administration. One of the consequences was that several armed bands were able to terrorize some of the areas under their control. The leader of one of these, a certain 'Chinese Chang', was captured by the rebels and executed after a 'short trial', along with a peasant who had raped a woman.

Guevara later conceded that *With hindsight, the methods we used in the Sierra may seem barbaric*. But he brushed aside all doubts by adding that *at the time the situation required an iron fist. We were forced to impose exemplary punishments to put a stop to breaches of discipline and root out nests of lawlessness that existed in all those areas lacking stable government.*[110]

Comandante Che Guevara

Immediately after the *Granma*'s ill-fated landing, press reports had triumphantly announced the deaths of Castro and Guevara. The *shadow army*, if the media were to be believed, had disappeared without trace. In an attempt to break through this wall of silence and disinformation, the rebels invited the veteran *New York Times* journalist Herbert L Matthews to find out about the war against Batista on the spot. An old hand who had been a reporter in the Spanish Civil War, Matthews knew Latin America like the back of his hand; disguising himself as a tourist, he made contact with the guerrillas who secretly led him to their camp.[111] He met Castro early in the morning of 17 February 1957 and found him an impressive interviewee. 'The man's personality is overwhelming', he wrote.

Matthews' report created a furore in the United States.[112] Suddenly, public curiosity in the rebels had been awakened, and from then on interest in the *barbudos*, who grew beards to distinguish themselves from the clean shaven or bestubbled *campesinos*, never slackened. On 23 April 1957 the journalist Bob Taber made the long climb from the plains up into the mountains, bringing with him a photographer. *The days went entirely according to plan; we tried to show the Americans our strength while deflecting any awkward questions.*[113]

One of the principal concerns for the Movement of 26 July (or M-26-7, named after the storming of the Moncada barracks on that day in 1953), was the lack of physical and political coordination in its struggle against the Batista dictatorship. Between the 'Sierra', the war of liberation in the mountains, and the 'Llano', the movement in the cities of the plains, there existed an enormous gulf. According to Guevara, *Links between the Llano and the Sierra had never been firm. Two basic factors were responsible for this: the geographical isolation of the Sierra and the differences of opinion concerning tactics and strategy that existed between the two groups.*[114]

The students and workers who were fighting the dictatorship

in the urban underground made no attempt to hide their suspicion of the movement's 'military' faction, personified by Castro and the guerrillas. They believed in civilian actions. However, those occasions when they did decide on armed resistance tended to end in a senseless loss of life; or so at least it seemed to the guerrillas.

An example of this was the storming of the Presidential Palace in Havana by the M-26-7-affiliated '*Directorio Revolucionario Estudiantil*' or Revolutionary Students' Directory, led by José Antonio Echeverría. This attempt to catch the lion in his den, as it were, failed tragically after some of the rebels became stuck in a traffic jam on the way to the coup, and the assailants entering the building then couldn't find the presidential suite were Batista had retired for lunch. The palace was quickly surrounded by police and soldiers and 35 rebels, Echeverría among them, paid for the disastrously failed coup with their lives.

Unconcealed distrust also prevailed between the guerrillas and the Communist '*Partido Socialista Popular*' (PSP), whose leaders rejected the policy of armed struggle. With the arrogance of those who know History's secret purpose, they distanced themselves from the guerrillas and a voluntaristic policy of rebellion that had no roots in the workers' movement, supporting instead a proletarian uprising. In their plans, Batista was to be driven from the Presidential Palace by a political general strike.

The 26 July Movement had certainly never refused to lend its support to such an uprising; indeed, a general strike was integral to their strategy. Castro, however, never managed to persuade his supporters in the cities to cooperate with the Communists, and he never managed to get them to effectively support the actions in the factories. The preparations were undermined by mutual enmities, with the result that the general strike of 9 April 1958 – *a tragic 9 April*, as Guevara called it – ended in fiasco. In the factories and ports work went on as usual, as the vast majority of trade unionists and Communists ignored the call for a strike.

This humiliating failure forced the 26 July Movement to reach a minimal consensus with less radical forces in the opposition, parties whose main concern was winning power rather than making revolution. Two of their spokesmen, Felipe Pazos and Raúl Chibás, deigned to leave their air-conditioned homes and travel into the sweltering heat of the mountains, where they tried to agree a programme for the post-Batista era.

The two sides drew up a joint declaration, the 'Manifesto of the Sierra of 12 July 1957'. It required its signatories to 'create a broad civil revolutionary front, to which all opposition parties, civil institutions and revolutionary forces should belong'. Under pressure to compromise, the negotiations produced an 'extremely moderate'[115] programme that put as much emphasis on political freedoms as it did on basic social rights.

The Manifesto of the Sierra of 12 July 1957 called on all Cubans to form a political revolutionary front 'to bring the brutal regime [...] to an end'. According to it, the only way to bring peace to Cuba was through free elections and a democratic government. The Manifesto specifically emphasised that the rebels were fighting 'for the high ideal of a free, democratic and just Cuba'. [...] Among other things, its programme called for the distribution of uncultivated land to landless workers. [...] Other items included measures to promote industrialisation and the abolition of gambling and corruption.

Hugh Thomas, 'Castro's Cuba'

Among other things, it announced the start of an intensive literacy campaign and the right of all citizens to state education. It promised to increase the pace of industrialisation, create new jobs and carry out a land reform in favour of smallholding peasants. The Manifesto contained no proposals for nationalising industry or collectivising agriculture. It is hardly surprising that many in the 26 July Movement disapproved of this shabby compromise. Later, Castro's critics would use it to attack him, accusing him of having betrayed the original principles and aims of the revolution.

Haydee Santamaria (front) and Celia Sanchez: two guerrillas who were to play an important role in Cuban politics after the revolution. Until her death in 1980, Celia Sanchez was one of Fidel Castro's closest companions and confidantes

The rebels had great difficulty overcoming the authoritarian instincts of the bourgeois opposition and the emigres, and persuading them that there could be no question of a provisional military junta coming to power after Batista's fall. The young rebels knew from Latin American history the peculiar dynamic of such military regimes, which had a tendency to develop unexpectedly into states within states. It was on precisely this issue that Castro had angrily attacked the 'Miami Pact' in his open letter of 14 December 1957. Agreed among Cuban opposition groups in Florida on 1 November, the Pact had provided for a military junta to preside over the transition period to democracy. Castro accused its supporters of 'deception'. He categorically demanded that, in the interests of the country, 'Cuba's civilian tradition be protected by its liberators as a precious inheritance'. He indignantly pointed out that the 26 July Movement had sent no delegates to represent it in Miami, angrily drew attention to its leading role in the armed struggle and made it plain that he was distancing himself from the anti-Batista forces of the Cuban bourgeoisie because of this.

As 1957 drew to a close, the rebels were strong enough to be able to press their claim to leadership. Florida was full of well-heeled Cuban gentlemen who spent their time impressing the ladies at cocktail parties with entertaining talk of armed resistance; they challenged the right of such people to be leading the revolution. Castro and his followers demanded that the revolution be led not from Miami but from the Sierra Maestra and the urban underground.[116]

It was on this basis that, on 20 July 1958, they agreed a new pact with the moderate opposition. The Caracas Accord, which would finally resolve all the complaints about weapons supply for the guerrillas and link their armed struggle to the civilian resistance, promised the restoration of democracy and the country's constitution. It also agreed a series of economic, social and institutional reforms to transform Cuban society. In so doing, all the signatories demanded that the United States no longer involve itself in Cuba's internal affairs.

Batista had good reason to rub his hands over the failure of the general strike of 9 April 1958. Disunity among the opposition had granted him a stay of execution, and once again he gambled everything on a single turn of the cards. He mobilized his entire armed forces to crush the revolutionary army once and for all. The operation that was to settle scores with the '*Fidelistas*' went by the name of 'Plan F-F', which could be interpreted either as *Fase Final* (Final Phase) or *Fin de Fidel* (End of Fidel).

On 25 May more than 10,000 men marched into the Sierra Maestra in what was intended to be a final offensive, aimed at crushing the guerrillas by deploying tanks and massive aerial bombardments. At first the rebels were forced to retreat before this enormously overwhelming force, but they soon regrouped and counterattacked. Morale among Batista's troops collapsed as their losses rose, and the number of deserters and turncoats increased. *Batista's army emerged from this last offensive on the Sierra Maestra with its back broken, but it wasn't yet defeated.*[117] Nevertheless, the circle around the Sierra Maestra was broken, and the cities of the plains now lay open to the guerrillas. They would pursue the army from east to west, bringing the island under their control bit by bit.

Together with his brother Raúl, Castro planned to surround the city of Santiago de Cuba. Camilo Cienfuegos, the archetype of the bearded rebel who had cultivated a striking resemblance to Jesus, was sent to the province of Pinar del Rio in the far west of the island. 'Comandante Che' was given the hardest task of all. He was to take the central province of Las Villas and break the communications between the west and the east of the island; a mission of tremendous strategic importance, which would be decisive for the outcome of the war.

The march west

On 31 August 1958 Guevara set out with the Army of Liberation's Eighth Column, the *'Ciro Redondo'*.[118] Once again, the mission was complicated by adverse circumstances. Instead of being able to travel in trucks or on horseback, the guerrillas had to make a forced march of several hundred kilometres on foot. They would endure extreme hardship before they arrived at their destination. *We marched through difficult, waterlogged terrain, constantly plagued by mosquitoes who made our moments of rest intolerable; we ate little and badly and drank water from marshy rivers or simply from swamps. Each day's march seemed to take longer, and became genuinely appalling. {...} Our lack of proper shoes was also sorely felt, and many men went through the swamps barefoot.*[119] It is almost miraculous that this army of ghosts, *that moved as if driven by some obscure psychological mechanism* (as Guevara had described their ragged forces back in December

1956), should not only have reached its destination but also challenged and what is more defeated Batista's army. Guevara's elevation to the pantheon of freedom fighters and his place as a luminous figure in history has its origins in the last act of the Cuban war of liberation.

On 29 December 1958 the decisive battle began for the provincial capital of Santa Clara, a major junction in the country's road and rail connections.[120] The guerrillas managed to fight their way into the city's residential area; their real target, however, was an armoured train with a *legendary* arsenal of weapons on board.

CHE GUEVARA
Extranjero pernicioso y Lider Comunista expulsado de la Argentina

CAMILO CIENFUEGOS
Lider Comunista

"Villaclareños"

Estos son los dos hombres que quieren llevar a nuestros jóvenes a la muerte y destruir nuestras riquezas.

Nosotros somos Cubanos y no Rusos.

¡LUCHEMOS CONTRA ELLOS!

JUVENTUD CIVICA CUBANA

'Citizens of Santa Clara: these are the two men who mean to drive our young people to their deaths and destroy our property. We are Cubans and not Russians. We must fight them!' Wanted poster for Che Guevara and Camilo Cienfuegos

Guevara's soldiers attacked the train at close quarters with Molotov cocktails. *Assailed by men throwing bottles of burning petrol from nearby positions, the train, being armour plated, turned into a veritable furnace for the soldiers inside. Within a few hours the entire garrison had surrendered and we found ourselves in possession of twenty-two wagons containing anti-aircraft guns, machine guns of the same make and the legendary stores of munitions.*[121]

After that is was only a matter of hours before the defenders surrendered, first in the barracks, then in the government buildings and the law court, and finally in the Grand Hotel, where they had kept the guerrillas under sniper fire until the bitter end. With the fall of Santa Clara the way to Havana was open. On 2 January, after Batista had fled the night before, Guevara entered the capital.

The hero of Santa Clara

From then on, his fame as a guerrilla was made, ensured by his fearlessness, selflessness and above all his almost superhuman strength of will. There were also his legendary military successes and his abilities as a thinker. In any discussion of the Cuban war of liberation Guevara's name is invariably associated with Santa Clara. It is there that an enormous and exceedingly ugly monument has been put up to him, and it his there that his mortal remains have been buried.

Victory celebrations in Havana

Che's 'golden years' in Cuba

Guevara was only 30 when he marched in triumph into Havana. His ascent within the revolutionary government would be just as triumphant. On 9 February 1959, having been honoured with the status of a 'native born' Cuban citizen,[122] he demanded an 'overwhelming influence over the course of the revolution'.[123] Che's meteoric rise to power has caused him to be described as the 'brains of the Castro regime'.[124] On 7 October 1959 he rose to become chief of the industrial section of the National Institute of Agrarian Reform (INRA), the 'nucleus of the real Cuban revolution'.[125] The position would become increasingly important as the agrarian reform that had been begun in the Sierra Maestra was extended to the rest of the country, carried out in two major steps, the first in May 1959 and the second in October 1963. For Che such reforms were an absolute precondition to any successful Latin American revolution. He rose to become full 'chief planner' and 'general manager' when he was appointed President of the National Bank

Guevara and Castro after the victory

on 26 November 1959, whereafter the banknotes bore his signature 'Che'; finally he took over the office of Industry Minister on 23 February 1961. However much criticism he later attracted for his economic dilettantism, his charisma remained undiminished. At the same time he was 'one of the most important originators of the revolution's radical course'.[127] Championing the cause of wealth redistribution, he energetically propounded an 'egalitarian Gospel' which among other things ensured lower rents and higher wages.

The burdens of power

Revolutionary justice

In a letter to Hilda of 28 January 1957 Che wrote, *I'm ready and thirsting for blood*.[129] No doubt the blood in question was that of the revolution's enemies, but it would still be being shed even after the rebels' victory. World opinion reacted with horror when, after the fall of Santiago de Cuba, Raúl Castro's men shot a hundred prisoners without trial and then went on to establish courts martial that contravened all the principles of the rule of law. Guevara was one of the participants in the summary justice.

Che's family had arrived 9 January 1959 as guests of the Revolution and were staying in the Hilton Hotel, but not even they were able to soften the 'Chief Prosecutor's' mood. As 'Commandant of La Cabaña', the military fortress that overlooks the entrance to Havana's harbour, Che had the task of 'putting on trial' various collaborators and war criminals of the Batista regime. At the time, more than a thousand prisoners were herded together in its cold, damp dungeons.

For evening after evening, trials were held behind the fortress walls. The courts sat from eight or nine o'clock onwards and were, almost without exception, presided over by lay judges, with a certain Orlando Borrego at their head, a 21-year-old accountant promoted by Che to be president of the court. He would later frankly testify that he had seen it as his task to impose 'a sense of revolutionary morality and justice'. It is clear the somewhat more impartial judges didn't have an easy job 'because there were prosecutors who were on the extreme left and [...] we had to restrain the ones who were always demanding a death penalty'.[130]

It is clear that efforts were made to gather evidence, hear witnesses – including witnesses for the defence – and take care in selecting the prosecutors and judges. Nevertheless, these were short trials, and they decided whether the defendant was to live or die. Sentence was handed down at about two or three o'clock in the morning, and often enough it was a sentence of death. A short while later the firing squads would start work. It is believed that several hundred executions were carried out this way.

'There are contradictory opinions about Che's role in the executions at La Cabaña. Several biographies by exiled oppositionists report that the Argentinian enjoyed the ritual of the firing squad and took pleasure in organising them, though they do admit that his orders came from Castro. Others report that Che was deeply troubled by the executions and pardoned as many prisoners as he could – although he did not hesitate to carry out orders that he considered justified.'[131]

When it came to 'cleansing' the army of those who had committed the most serious crimes, Che was without mercy. When it came to defending the revolution he had no scruples, since for him the revolution came before everything else – including the right to life. When his Mexican friend Dr David Mitriani was visiting him for the celebrations of 26 July 1959, he expressed

Chronicle of Events

01.01.1959 Batista flees – Castro enters Santiago

17.05.1959 First Agrarian Reform

13.02.1960 First trade agreement with the Soviet Union

19.10.1960 The United States begins its trade embargo

03.01.1961 Diplomatic relations between the USA and Cuba are broken off

16.04.1961 The socialist character of the revolution is announced

17.04.1961 Bay of Pigs invasion

25.01.1962 Cuba withdraws from the OAS

October 1962 Missile Crisis

13.10.1963 Second Agrarian Reform

shock and incomprehension at the summary executions of the *Batistianos*; Che casually replied, *Look, in these situations it's either kill them or they kill you.*[132]

The revolutionaries may have had good reasons for using the law to bring about a general settling of accounts, for example the fact that about 20,000 Cubans had been murdered by the dictatorship's accomplices, some of them in the most savage way imaginable. In 1959 people across the entire island were taking the law into their own hands with campaigns of reprisals, and this needed to be stopped. To an extent, the regime did manage to stop it. Nevertheless, the short trials and the executions remained a stain upon the revolution's and the revolutionaries' first days, and upon Guevara himself.[133]

'Chief theorist of Fidelism'

As we know, Che had declared himself a Communist when in prison in Mexico. It was, however, still a long way to go from self-declared Communist to Marxist theorist; he didn't become the latter until 1963/64, when he took part in the famous 'planning debate' with 'professional' European Marxists. Che's writings up until then show his transition from studious autodidact of Marxism to ideological head of the revolution, to 'brain of the Castro regime' and 'chief theorist of 'Fidelism'.[134] In this capacity he exercised an overwhelming influence on the Cuban revolution.[135]

Che's profession of Communism while in prison in Mexico and Fidel's indignant reaction to it already give some idea of the ideological differences between the two revolutionary leaders. From the beginning of the war of liberation Che expressed his Marxist convictions ever more clearly, while Fidel avoided even mentioning the word 'socialism'. Castro wanted to lend the revolution a 'moderate facade',[136] partly because he was more inclined towards social democracy – a fact that's evident in 'History will absolve me',[137] the famous speech he gave at his trial in 1953 – but partly

In April 1959 Castro accepted an American newspaper publisher's invitation to visit the United States. This 'goodwill trip' turned into a high-profile political event. Fidel's comrades prepared a big welcome for him on his return

also because he didn't want to alert the USA to his plans. Che on the other hand was too much the missionary ever to hide his convictions.

Castro had more than once vehemently denied the socialist character of the revolution. When the *Chicago Tribune*'s Caracas correspondent Jules Dubois questioned him about this in an interview that was broadcast over the rebels' own radio, he took great pains to lay to rest suspicions about his Communist activities. Dubois asked Castro several times whether he was a Communist sympathiser. 'Fidel replied that Batista had spread this rumour in order to get weapons from the US, and declared he had no intention whatsoever of nationalising industry or the private sector.'[138]

On 16 January 1959 Fidel had vigorously challenged claims that he was really a Communist. While travelling across the United States in April, he wearily denied reporters' repeated insinuations to this effect. In May, when the agrarian reform was causing controversy, especially in the United States, he was still talking about a third way between capitalism ('that kills people with hunger') and Communism (that suppressed the freedoms 'human beings hold so dear'). He calmed doubters who saw Cuba already drifting towards Communism by pointing out that the colour of the revolution was not red but olive green, the olive green of the rebel army's uniform.[139]

It wasn't until April 1961 and invasion by American mercenaries in the Bay of Pigs that he finally showed his hand and declared Cuba a socialist society. Then on 1 December he made a profession of political faith that was to delight the East as much as it shocked the West. 'I am a Marxist-Leninist,' he announced, 'and I shall remain a Marxist-Leninist to the day I die.'[140] It is still unclear whether this shift from officially denying socialism to openly declaring it was an example of Castro's pragmatism or his tactical calculation as a statesman.

Guevara, then 'only' a minister and President of the National Bank, was much more open about his ideological convictions, and this had its consequences. Most anti-Communists in the USA and in Cuba itself considered Guevara the most important advocate of the island's 'subjugation' to the Soviet Union, and despised him as the 'red' flea in Fidel's ear.[141] And indeed, Che acted from the beginning as an orthodox Communist. When the conflict with the United States escalated and rapprochement with the Soviet Union came onto the agenda, he showed himself to be 'a prisoner of Neanderthal Marxism'.[142]

Cuba's journey into the Soviet sphere of influence began in the autumn of 1959, and as the member of the regime most strongly orientated towards Communism Che played a major part in it.

Many of the preliminary negotiations proceeded under his 'command'. During a long goodwill tour, Che first contacted the Soviets in Cairo, where he wanted to discuss a particularly delicate subject, namely sugar. In order to punish Cuba the United States had refused to import any more of its crop, and other buyers now had to be found.

In the event, the Soviet Union said it was prepared to buy half a million tonnes of Cuba's sugar, and thus began the first stage in a long and tense relationship between the two countries. Henceforth, envoys from the Kremlin regularly came to Havana. The most important of these was Anastas Mikoyan, acting Chairman of the Soviet Union's Council of Ministers, who visited Havana for talks in late January 1960. On 13 February 1960 the revolutionary government concluded its first trade and credit agreement with the Soviets. To some extent the Soviet Union took over what had been the role of the United States; it undertook to buy a million tonnes of sugar a year between 1960 and 1964, and it granted the Cubans a $100 million loan with a twelve-year repayment period at 2.5 per cent interest.

Guevara with Nikita Kruschev, Moscow, October 1960

Guevara, now considered by Moscow the 'main architect of Soviet-Cuban economic cooperation', returned Mikoyan's visit in the autumn of the same year. 'When Che arrived in Moscow on an official visit, [...] his purpose was to ratify and extend Soviet-Cuban cooperation', and in this he succeeded. 'He left Moscow on 16 November with his admiration for the motherland of socialism undimmed. [...] This was to be the high point in his love affair with real existing socialism.'[143]

China's man in Havana?

A complete newcomer to the international socialist stage, Che found his political sympathies changing after a Congress of the world's 81 Communist and Workers' Parties had given him some insight into the rancours and intrigues existing within the 'family of Communist Parties'. 'From being one of the Soviet Union's most passionate defenders, he became one of its harshest critics.'[144] 'Scarcely six years lay between his letter from the Sierra Maestra (to René Ramos Latour, leader of the 26 July Movement) in which he spoke admiringly of the countries behind the "Iron Curtain" (and which he later described as 'idiotic'), and the stinging criticisms he made of the USSR and other Eastern European countries in 1964-65.'[145]

More than any other event, the missile crisis of October 1962 cast a shadow over Che's relations with the Soviet Union. He was enraged that Khrushchev should have retreated in the face of Kennedy's threats, but that he should have done so without consulting his Cuban 'comrades' he considered unforgivable. In an interview with the British journalist Sam Russell he went so far as to make the chilling admission that, had they been under their control, the Cubans would have launched the missiles.[146] As for nuclear weapons, this apocalyptic conclusion can be found among Guevara's thoughts on 'Tactics and Strategy in the Latin American Revolution' of autumn 1962. *We remain convinced that*

Guevara and Mao Zedong, China, 1 December 1960

the we must stay on the road to liberation even if it means millions dying in a nuclear war.[147] The Soviet Union's 'betrayal' during the missile crisis was something Guevara never got over.

As his doubts about the Soviet model of economic management grew, his criticisms of the Russian 'Big Brother' became ever more polemical. By 1963 he had lost his faith in the Soviet model, while his affinity towards Beijing was growing. The Chinese route to socialism seemed to him to be the better one. Given that political and economic relations between Cuba and the so-called fraternal socialist countries were increasingly imposing a 'division of labour' detrimental to the 'Red Island's' interests, Che was right to have reservations about Moscow. But he could hardly have been surprised by the severity of the Kremlin's reaction to his 'deviationism' and heresy. At the time of internal socialist schism between Moscow and Beijing, anyone publicly declaring his sympathies for the Chinese route to socialism could in

Moscow's eyes only be a Maoist, an extremist, or still worse, a Trotskyist, anarchist, utopian or adventurer.

Later, when the joke was making the rounds that Che was 'China's man' in Havana, it would be time for him to end his political marriage with the Cuban revolution.[148]

The 'New Man'

In an interview with Maurice Zeitlin Guevara made the uncharacteristically modest statement, *I'm not used to theorising. I prefer practice to theory*.[149] That was in 1961, a good two years after he and his comrades had descended to the plains and taken power in Cuba. By then he was effectively both: practitioner and theorist, and probably had been for some time. He even became known as the 'theoretical head of the revolution', whose theories had been influenced, indeed dominated, by his experiences in the war of liberation.

This was especially true of his concept of the 'new man'. Guevara's ideas on this had been shaped by the experience of two long years of war. His personal experiences of the adversities encountered by the revolution and its attempt to transform peoples' consciousness had a profound influence on his theoretical imagination. Put simply, the kind of life that the guerrillas, and especially Guevara himself, had led during the struggle anticipated and exemplified the qualities that would distinguish the 'new man'. *It was the first time in history when people undertook important tasks or dangerous missions for no other reward than the knowledge they were doing their duty. In our work of revolutionary education we often come to speak on this instructive subject. The mentality among our fighters anticipated that of the man of the future*.[150]

Selflessness, solidarity, altruism, a sense of responsibility, conscientiousness in doing one's duty, a strong moral motivation – all these were the virtues that Guevara ascribed the revolutionary. Once they had been carefully instilled in the individual, they would also shape the 'new man'. To do this, *society must in its entirety be transformed into a gigantic school.*[151] These virtues needed to be taught from childhood, starting with the Communist youth organisations and going on through universities, workplaces and the Party. *The reward*, Che promised, *is a new society in which people will be motivated differently – the society of the Communist man.*[151] It would be a society that exemplified neither to the ideas of the nineteenth century nor to those of the 'decadent and sick' twentieth.

Guevara found himself having to deal with objections that building socialism meant sacrificing the individual on the altar of the state, or indeed the altar of collectivism. As it was, he uncompromisingly insisted that *individualism as such, the isolated behaviour of individuals within their social environment, must disappear in Cuba,*[153] and he called on the individual to see himself *as the least important cog in the machine.* But he also thought that he could, at least in principle, more than compensate the individual for this mechanical and somewhat inhuman functionality; *The fact is that the individual feels more fulfilled by having much greater inner rewards and much more responsibility.*[154] Acutely aware that many people feared an egalitarian society would be dehumanising, he reassured them by pointing out that *despite their apparent standardisation, in socialism human beings are more complete; although we still lack a perfected mechanism for it, people's opportunities for expressing themselves and making their mark on society are infinitely greater.*[155]

For Guevara, 'the first and last task of the revolution was to create a new man, a Communist man, as the dialectical negation of the individual in capitalist society'.[156] The task was to win the Darwinian struggle for survival against a winner-takes-all society of merciless competition in which everyone puts himself first. In contrast to 'rapacious human beings living in a rapacious society',

Guevara continues to be held in special reverence in Cuba to this day. 'Ser como el Che!' ('I want to be like Che!') is a slogan taught to Cuba's children in primary school.

Bert Hoffmann

the monstrous progeny of the capitalist system, the Argentinian-Cuban revolutionary outlined his figure of the 'new man'.

Guevara spoke enthusiastically of the great and beautiful experiment of *building a new Cuba*,[157] a socialist society whose final aim was to create a society that was classless. He bluntly announced that *to build Communism we must create a new man at the same time as we create a new material basis for society*.[158] He declared the most important indices of this construction to be developing socialist consciousness and increasing production. It was to be a dialectical relationship in which each factor would stimulate the other, although the development of consciousness would dominate.

The leading thinker of the revolution was acutely aware of the vast discrepancy between this aspiration and the harsh reality of working life. In his

The Minister for Industry at a textile factory

meetings with core supporters – with young Communists, students, professors or workers – the issue of lack of work discipline almost always came up. The Minister for Industry knew of countless cases of absenteeism, laziness and negligence in the factories and offices. Despite this, Guevara stuck to ideas about social psychology that, given the realities of everyday working life, seem almost bizarre. *Something extraordinary has happened*, he declared in 1963, *namely the complete transformation of consciousness among the masses, and this after only a few years of revolutionary activity*.[159]

The task the theoretical head of the Cuban revolution had given himself was twofold, and each side of it was equally challenging: *We are fighting poverty, but at the same time we're also fighting alienation. One of Marxism's fundamental aims is to abolish 'private interest' and profit as factors of psychological motivation. Much as Marx was concerned with economic factors, he was equally concerned with the effect of these factors on human thinking itself. This he called 'consciousness'. If Communism stops being concerned with consciousness, then it might amount to a method of distribution, but never a revolutionary ethic.*[160]

Here the naturalised Cuban, who had renounced dogmatism many times himself, was embracing a social philosophy that quite clearly made thought the child of desire; the desire in question being to initiate a transformation in consciousness by proclaiming a socialist society. But why should accepting the highly abstract notion of being collective owners of their factory encourage workers to behave altruistically, or with greater solidarity, or to achieve high levels of economic performance, when the act of nationalisation had barely changed anything in their living and working conditions? As it was, the pressure to increase productivity actually tended to increase after the revolution.

Only an inveterate idealist like Guevara could have been surprised and disappointed when enthusiasm among Cubans often left so much to be desired, or when their human weaknesses failed to exemplify the revolution's grand ideals. Faced with this, Che would boast of great transformations in society that quite obviously hadn't taken place. *In today's Cuba, work is becoming increasingly rewarding for people in a way it never had before, and a new source of joy.* Guevara invited anyone who didn't believe him to come and help with the '*Zafra*' or sugar cane harvest (something he himself did regularly) so that *they can see how lovingly and gracefully our women cut the sugar cane.*[161] Guevara gave himself and his comrades no lesser task than ensuring that *every worker is in love with his factory.*[162]

He was a champion of 'voluntary' work, vigorously promoting it in the belief that it more than anything would help raise social

Che as a machetero, voluntary worker on the sugar cane harvest, circa 1963

consciousness. He joined the 'red battalions', whose members would scour the country in search of regular daily work in an effort to speed up development, working in building sites, factories or fields. He called on Cubans to be ready for the heroic task of *working every day of the year*.[163] According to Guevara, it was in 'voluntary work', which he considered especially valuable as 'a school for raising consciousness', that the 'new man' would first take shape. Some may have noticed that many Cubans' participation in the '*domingos rojos*' or 'red Sundays' was semi-voluntary at best, and inspired not by revolutionary enthusiasm but by social pressure from neighbours or fellow workers; Guevara, however, evidently chose not to see this. The 'new man' he championed was evidently a strange creature. He was a purely theoretical human being whose psyche combined both social sensibilities and the more traditional virtues, of a kind typical even for authoritarian societies. He was a prototype made to a blueprint, a test tube creation, abstract and artificial. He could survive no direct contact with reality.

Also remarkable is the missionary fervour that accompanied Guevara's belief in secular salvation, and his conviction that History's end point had almost been achieved.

America admires us;[164] of this the *comandante* was certain. As though borrowing from North American myths of Providence that had imagined the United States as the 'New Jerusalem' or the 'House on the Hill', he glorified the Cuban Revolution as the mirror, the lighthouse or the burning torch for America. As an 'engineer of the human soul', the 'new man', as Che had designed him was to serve as a similarly shining example for Latin Americans, and not only for them.

Married to the revolution

Che wasn't brilliantly qualified for his new jobs. While he had some knowledge of industrial management, he had nothing else in the way of practical economic experience. Indeed, after he was appointed President of the National Bank on 26 November 1959, a revealing joke went about; Castro, it was said, had asked at a meeting of the Cuban leadership whether they had any volunteers for President of the Central Bank, whether anyone present was an 'economist'. Che, who had dozed off, thought he'd heard him say 'a communist', and put his hand up.[165]

Che tried to make up for the gaps in his knowledge by working with Sisyphean determination. The Ministry for Industry became a sort of school of economic policy, operating as a hive of constant activity. Foreign guests came to visit, 'revolution tourists' among them. Guerrilla commanders sought the minister's company in order to be able to bask in the reflected glory of his power. Often enough they found him unavailable; Guevara was, like Castro to this day, very much a night owl. He was known to receive visitors at five o'clock in the morning, and discuss complex matters with them until it was almost midday. On top of this there were statistics to study, reports to check, articles to write, instructions to give, speeches to draft and much else. It seemed as if Guevara worked a 24-hour day. His admirers Jean-Paul Sartre and Simone de Beauvoir remarked of the monstrous workload undertaken by Che and other revolutionaries that 'one might have thought that sleep had abandoned them, that it too had emigrated to Miami'.

It is astonishing that someone like Che, who had grown up in a fairly stable family and had been especially close both to his mother and his youngest brother Juan Martin, should have so consciously extricated himself from this network of emotional ties once he became a revolutionary. There were already signs of this happening during the war of liberation; on one occasion, he had contacted his mother over a radio transmitter to tell her about his 'adventures' in the Sierra Maestra. At first their difficulties communicating seemed only to be technical ones; but his mother followed up their conversation by writing him a tender letter on his thirtieth birthday. 'Dear Teté', she wrote, 'I was so happy to hear your voice after such a long time. I didn't recognise it at all – you seem to have become a different person. Perhaps it was a bad connection, or perhaps you've changed. It wasn't until you called me "old lady" that I was able to hear your old voice again.'[166]

It is true that Che saw his parents several more times, first in Havana and then at the Conference in Punta del Este in August 1961, but he had decided once and for all to cut all personal ties, dedicate himself entirely to the revolution. So it was that his contacts with home became increasingly rare and distant.

In a letter he wrote to his 'Dear Vieja', his 'dear old lady', from India he records how his sense of mission and of having some other purpose in life than its ordinary comforts had cut him off from his past. He wrote, *In the meantime I've come to realise something about the tension between the enormous task ahead of me and my private life. I'm still the same loner I always was, finding my way without help from anyone; but I know now my historical duty. I have no country, no wife, no children, no parents, no brothers and sisters; my friends are my friends only so long as they share my political beliefs. And yet I'm happy, for I'm learning something about myself; not just the powerful inner strength I've always felt, but also the ability to lead others and the absolutely fatalistic sense of mission that leaves me fearing nothing.*[167]

Che became distant from his family, contributing to the impression that he'd been drawn into the revolution's exclusive enchanted circle. So completely had he dedicated himself to its demands that he didn't once visit his beloved mother in the days before she died on 16 May 1965.

Had she been able to read minds, Hilda Gadea would undoubtedly have left Che, having been deeply hurt by him. Deep down he must have been so against getting any closer to her – in other words, marrying her – that he could barely hide his aversion. In any case, his behaviour towards her was unworthy of him, and bordered on disrespect.

On 26 July 1955 Fidel and his followers celebrated the second anniversary of the storming of the Moncada barracks in Mexico City's Chapultepec Park. After the festivities and speeches a small group of them went back to a friend's apartment to have supper. While Fidel cooked *spaghetti al vongole* the exiles chatted animatedly among each other. Che was conspicuously silent in the midst of all the talk, causing Fidel to ask him complacently, 'Hey, Che, why are you so quiet? Is it because your minder is here?' He meant of course Hilda; the remark is very revealing about how she was seen by the rebels.

Che never stood up for her; and he himself wasn't sure how he felt about her. No doubt he'd have really liked to walk out on her in classic macho style, had Hilda not by then become pregnant. Che clearly vacillated between the bourgeois conventions he still hadn't abandoned and his desire to live the freedom he had won to the full. He decided to marry Hilda, although not without entrusting his conflicting feelings to his diary. *For someone else it might be one of the great moments in their life*, he wrote, *but for me the whole business is rather painful. I'm going to be a father, and in a few days I'm going to marry Hilda. For her this decision was a dramatic one; for me it was hard. She's finally getting what she wants – though only for the time being as far as I'm concerned, even if she hopes it'll be for good.*[168]

Che Guevara and Hilda Gadea Acosta wed on 18 August 1955 at the register office of the little town of Tepotzotlán, on the outskirts of the capital. In no sense did the ceremony mark the beginning of married life for them. The couple remained distant from each other, albeit – given Guevara's years in the Sierra Maestra – sometimes by necessity.

The fact is that he was, as the saying goes, married to the revolution. This was something that Aleida March de la Forre was also to learn. Che met her for the first time during the western campaign; a strikingly beautiful 22-year-old who was helping to supply the half-starved partisans with food. She very clearly had nothing in common with the stereotyped role that Che had envisaged for women in the war of liberation, namely that of helpers who would carry messages for the guerrillas by day and lovingly prepare meals for the weary fighters in the evening. Instead, Aleida shouldered a rifle and followed her lover into battle. This is also how she thought of herself; as a comrade in arms, and not as some groupie of his.

At the end of January 1959 Hilda arrived in Havana with her three-year-old daughter Hildita. Instead of meeting them at the airport himself, Che sent his friend Dr Oscar Fernández Mell – an indication of how awkward he felt. Nevertheless, he was strong enough in the end to tell her the truth and admit that he was living with another woman. In her memoirs Hilda records how deeply Che's admission hurt her. 'My pain was great, but we agreed to follow our convictions and divorce.'[169]

On 3 June 1959 Aleida and Che married in the bride's home town of Santiago de Las Vegas. 'After the simple ceremony in the registry office, the two of them gave a party [...] Raúl came with

Che and Aleida Guevara March, shortly after their wedding, 1959

his wife Vilma Espín. Camilo turned up with a lot of noise and a lot of rum to "liven up" the party. Aleida was wearing a new white dress that suited her well, while Che as always was wearing his olive green uniform and black beret.'[170]

The marriage produced four children: first Aleidita, then in 1962 their first son Camilo, Celia a year later and finally Ernesto. It is difficult to say whether Che was a good father; he was too conspicuous by his absence. His revolutionary duties meant that he barely ever got to see his children. His appearances at number 772, 47th Street, Nuevo-Vedado, where his family lived, were rather more the exception than the rule. No sooner had he embraced his children and asked them how they were than it was almost time for him to leave again. 'He was never home', his daughter complained.[171]

Aleida had imagined their future together quite differently. She had no intention of becoming 'the wife at his side' – she was far too self-confident and headstrong for that – but not even this role was offered her. At first she had still accompanied Che on his journeys across Cuba, but later she found herself ever more frequently left at home, alone with the children for increasingly longer periods of time. Over the winter of 1964-65, for example, she had to wait four and a half months for him to return.

When he was at home, Aleida and the children came to feel some of stubbornness and his strict morality. He expected the whole family to adopt his ascetic way of life. In order that there should be not the slightest suggestion that he was claiming material privileges for himself, he demanded from his family that they live extremely simply. One day Aleida called him to ask to borrow his official car to go shopping in town. He replied by reminding her, *No, Aleida, no, you know that the car isn't mine, it belongs to the government, and that's why you can't use it. You must take the bus like everyone else.*[172]

From his journeys abroad he brought back sackloads of presents, but never kept any of the jewellery, paintings, statues and various electrical appliances for himself, donating them instead to youth training centres. As a result his home remained sparsely furnished. It reminded Che's old Argentinian friend Ricardo Rojo of the room he had rented in La Paz, where the only furniture was a nail in the wall that served as his wardrobe.[173]

In early 1959 Che's doctors advised him to take some time off to convalesce in quiet surroundings, and a confiscated villa in Tarara, on the outskirts of Havana, was lent to him for this purpose. He was subsequently enraged to find himself accused of living a life of luxury there by the magazine *Revolucion*. The fact was that lounging around all day was the last thing he did at this temporary home; instead, he dictated his experiences from the war of liberation onto a tape recorder, and held meetings every evening with members of a project group for agrarian reform that had been set up by Castro.

Guevara at his son Camilo's first birthday party

He neither would nor could leave unchallenged this accusation of a life of privilege and ease, and on 10 March the *Revolucion* published his withering reply. *I would like to inform readers of the Revolucion*, he wrote, *that I am sick and that my illness was contracted not in the course of frequenting casinos and nightclubs but of dedicating myself to the revolution beyond the limits of my own physical stamina. {...} I promise {...} the people of Cuba that I shall leave this house as soon as I am well again {...}. Che.*[174]

Che saw his wife and children for the last time in October 1966; the one child notable by her absence at the meeting was Hildita, whose presence was considered a 'security risk'. Che's eldest child was by then ten years old, and since Che was already wearing his camouflage suit in preparation for his journey to Bolivia, Hildita, it was thought, might see through this more easily than her siblings and mention this unusual meeting with her father to others.[175]

In his letter of farewell to his children Hildita, Aleidita, Camilo, Celia and Ernesto, Guevara admits to not having spent enough time with them as a father. Perhaps this is why he so insistently invoked the revolutionary virtues that for him had always taken precedence over the conventions of family life. *Should you ever have to read this letter,* he wrote, *then it will be because I am no longer among you. You will scarcely be able to remember me, and the youngest of you won't be able to remember me at all. Your father is a man who acted as he believed, and has no doubt that he who has remained true to his convictions. Become good revolutionaries. Learn much, so that you can master the technology that enables us to master Nature. {...} Always be ready to feel every injustice keenly, wherever and against whomever it is done. That is the finest quality a revolutionary can have. Farewell children; I hope I shall see you again. A big kiss and a hug from Dad.*[176]

He left his family to the care of the socialist state. *I don't regret,* he wrote to Fidel, *that I leave behind no material wealth for my wife and children. In fact, I am glad to be doing so. I ask nothing for them, for I know that the state will provide for their care and upbringing.*

Cuba's travelling salesman

Although Che's official duties, first as President of the National Bank and then as Minister for Industry, formally tied him to his office in Havana, he travelled a remarkably great deal – always for the purpose of promoting the Cuban revolution and securing promises of help. In summer 1959 for example he was away for three months travelling in African and Asian states and in Yugoslavia, while in October 1960 he visited Czechoslovakia, the Soviet Union, China, North Korea, East Germany and Hungary at the head of an economic delegation. In March 1964 he travelled to Geneva to give a speech before UNCTAD, the World Trade Conference; and then of course there was his brilliant appearance in New York before the General Assembly of the United Nations in mid-November 1964.

As Cuba's representative at the World Trade Conference in Geneva, 1964

However, his most important journey took him onto home territory; the Uruguayan seaside resort of Punta del Este, from where he made a lightning visit to Buenos Aires. It was in fashionable Punta del Este that the Inter-American Economic and Social Conference held its first meeting on 6 August 1961 to discuss John F Kennedy's 'Alliance for Progress' plan. Announced by Kennedy on 13 March, the plan was supposedly aimed at helping Latin America 'throw off the chains of poverty'; in reality though it was a rival programme to Fidelism, and Guevara was determined not to miss the opportunity of raising the Cuban flag at this forum.

It was winter in Punta del Este when Che arrived there. A violent asthma attack laid him low at precisely the moment an immense programme of work awaited him. It was clear that he and the Cuban delegation were to be the main objects of attention both for the participants at the conference and world public opinion. He was constantly besieged by hordes of journalists, leaving other ministers standing sourly on the sidelines. While they were elegantly dressed in suits and ties, Che wore his uniform; and his speeches were as militant as his appearance. On 8 August he read the riot act to the North American politicians who had promised their southern 'cousins' $20 billion in loans spread over 10 years. It was clear that this was nothing other than a lure to immunise Latin America's politicians against the temptations of the Cuban revolution. It was equally clear that the USA would use it to make the subcontinent even more dependent than it already was.[177]

But Che did not stop at bitterly denouncing US policy; he went on to present the Latin Americans with a list of basic demands they should be making of the United States: 'The freedom to export their raw materials wherever they wanted; an end to the USA's protectionist policies, which subsidised their own products and thus made any real competition impossible; and help towards industrialising the economies of the Latin American countries – the cornerstone of economic independence and prosperity.' In the light of today's globalisation debate, the list seems a remarkably modern one.[178]

Che called on the USA to allow Cuba the right to 'be different', and demanded a non-aggression pact. Given that the Bay of

Pigs had happened less than six months earlier, this might not seem an unreasonable request. He promised the USA *{...} that we will not export the revolution, we guarantee that not a single gun will leave Cuba, not a single weapon will leave Cuba to be used in another Latin American country*, on condition that the United States respect Cuban sovereignty.

The appeal fell on deaf ears. One after the other, the countries of Latin America broke off relations with Cuba under Washington's pressure. At the end of January 1962 the Organisation of American States (OAS) decided to expel Cuba from its ranks. In February Kennedy tightened the USA's existing trade embargo on the country.[179]

Che didn't only mix with diplomats and journalists in Punta del Este; he also attended some high-level meetings. The Argentinian President Arturo Frondizi wanted to meet him for talks, and on 18 August Che flew to Buenos Aires, where he found a small escort awaiting him under the command of an army colonel. The colonel's orders had been vague: merely that he was to pick up an important visitor from the airport. 'When the door of the airplane opened he was extremely surprised to see a bearded man in a green uniform jump to the ground, his coat unbuttoned and a glittering commandant's star pinned to his beret. [...]'[180] His consternation increased when he recognised Che's face; mute with fright, he doffed his cap twice. Unprompted, Che offered him his hand in greeting and introduced himself to the man with military brevity, *I am Comandante Guevara, Colonel. Am I right in thinking that's your car?*

Guevara and the Argentinian President fell into passionate debate over the future of Latin America, especially of the Cuban revolution and Argentina, until the president's wife and daughter called them to lunch. This was steak '*a caballo*', grilled beef with roast potatoes and hard-boiled eggs – something Che, as a native Argentinian, could not resist.

In the meantime, word had got round of his visit to Buenos Aires. Unrest began to grow in the capital, although by then Guevara was already on his way back to Montevideo. From there he went on to Brasilia, where he received the order of the '*Cruziero do Sul*' (Cross of the South) from President Janio da Silva Quadros. Guevara and Quadros discussed concerns that Cuba might join the Warsaw Pact and renounce representative democracy for good, and in so doing throw away any chance of entering the Organisation of Inter-American States. The gamble of talking to a political outcast like Che at a time when anti-Communist hysteria against Cuba was reaching the most bizarre heights cost both presidents their office. Quadros was forced to resign only a week later; Frondizi received a stay of execution, but was out of office within seven months.

In his second speech at Punta del Este, on 16 August, Guevara appeared much more conciliatory towards the USA. He emphasised that *We have always been prepared to reconcile our differences with the United States {...}*.[181] To many delegates this announcement sounded so very promising that the Argentinian and Brazilian governments took it upon themselves to bring Guevara and Richard N Goodwin, Kennedy's foremost personal assistant, around the table together. Che went out of his way to be charming, having a box of the finest Havana cigars sent up to Goodwin's room as a gesture of goodwill. Unknown to all but a few, Che and Goodwin met secretly at two o'clock in the morning of 17 August while a birthday celebration was going on outside the Congress. Once Che – as always, ravenous – had finished off a 'heavy cream cake', the talks could begin.

Che repeated the offers he had made the day before. Cuba, he stressed, was interested in talking to the USA and in finding a solution to their common problems. Remarkably, he offered to abandon any of the 'alliances with the East' that he himself had helped engineer. He also hinted that Cuba would be willing to end its revolutionary intrigues in Latin America. In return, he demanded first of all that Washington refrain from any attempt to violently overthrow the Cuban revolution, and second that it lift its economic sanctions against the island and recognise the new 'socialist' Cuban government.

The talks ended shortly before six in the morning. On his return to Washington, Goodwin reported to Kennedy on his secret talks with Guevara and was instructed to draft a memorandum of them. The record of this remarkable discussion disappeared into the filing cabinets, and nothing further came of it.[182]

Breaking out of underdevelopment

Situated in the United States' 'backyard', Cuba had been exploited by that country's corporations for decades, with the result that it wasn't nearly as deeply and hopelessly mired in underdevelopment as most Latin American countries. There was no denying that the island had modernised to some extent, and its growth rates weren't nearly as low as elsewhere in the Third World. It had one crucial flaw, though: the developed sectors of its economy and its modern infrastructure were heavily concentrated around Havana, where large US corporations controlled the telephone, transport and energy systems, not to mention the banking and tourist industries.

Agro-business controlled the countryside, growing vast fields of sugarcane. This lucrative branch of industry had deformed Cuba's economy into a dominant monoculture, leaving it at the mercy of a terms of trade dictated by the United States and the world market. Cuba's prosperity was utterly dependent on the world price of sugar, which would rise and fall precipitately and erratically.

The few inhabitants of the Cuban countryside who were able to find work as '*macheteros*' during the sugar harvest, in what was genuinely back-breaking work, had to survive as best they could during the 'dead time' that followed the end of the season.

Smallholders struggling to make a living on *minifundas* could barely feed themselves on what they produced. For Cuba as for most other Latin American countries, a catastrophic gap between town and country was the norm. Then there was the fact that the country had been a supplier of raw materials to industrialised economies and a market for their manufactured goods since the sixteenth century, and the roots of this economic role ran deep.

There was then a very great deal for the revolutionaries to do, given that they not only wanted to end the dictatorship and establish a new political system but also change society. This was particularly true for Guevara, who was considered the 'brain' of the revolution.[183] Though he worked tirelessly on economic issues – first as chief of the industry department of the INRA (National Agra-reform Institute) from 7 October 1959, then as President of the National Bank from 26 November 1959, and finally as Minister for Industry from 23 February 1961 – in the end the difficulties proved too much for him. With his dreams of building a Communist society and a 'realm of freedom', he was perceived as an enthusiast both out of touch with economic rationality and drastically unsuited to his job.

What he would most liked to have done is transform Cuba into a modern industrial society by a sort of secular act of creation. By the middle of October 1960 almost the whole of industry had been nationalised on his initiative.[184] He went so far as to make the development of science and technology 'central to how he conceived of society'.[185] Based purely on theory, his wildly ambitious economic predictions went far beyond the actual and characteristically backward state of the country's economic relations. *In the beginning*, he confidently claimed, *productivity could be increased by rationalising production. {...} Then an ever more complete mechanisation will be necessary {...} Finally we will need to introduce the more or less gradual automisation of all production processes, in other words, fully enter the field of electronics. It might be objected that this is one of the newest and most complicated sectors of industry and that only a few countries have mastered it. Our view is that this is yet another reason for speeding up research and development in this sector. The world is about to enter the electronic age. {...} Everything indicates that this science will become a yardstick of a country's economic development.*[186]

The prediction would prove to be a remarkably far-sighted one. But it was also a vision of industrialisation, rationalisation, mechanisation and finally computerisation for a country that, in the years after 1959, was plagued by a host of very basic economic problems: war damage, the US-American economic embargo, acts of sabotage, an exodus of skilled workers such as technicians and engineers, shortages of spare parts, lack of capital for necessary investments and so on and so forth. Despite this, the revolutionaries' first development strategy for 1961 to 1963, which Guevara had a big hand in drafting, planned to diversify agriculture while scaling back sugar production and increasing the pace of industrialisation. Its ultimate aim was to replace with domestic products, and in as short a time as possible, the expensive imports that were draining the country's foreign currency reserves.

Many of the bottlenecks, shortages and deficits in the economy were exacerbated by the fact that the amateur economists around Guevara had to proceed on the principle of trial and error. On top of this, the untutored planners had to come up with an outline for import-substitution industrialisation from scratch. Given Cuba's level of economic development at the time, this proved to be an expensive and essentially unaffordable illusion. Guevara paid a heavy price for trying to accelerate industrialisation and scale back sugar production; productivity fell dramatically, and the economy was paralyzed by a wave of strikes.[187]

As a result, the revolutionaries resorted to a new strategy after 1963. Their ambitious industrialisation plans now gave priority to agriculture, and above all to the sugar sector that had been neglected for ideological reasons. Meanwhile a more modest industrial

Sugar refinery chimneys, a common sight in Cuba

sector would be based on servicing agriculture, producing fertilizers, agricultural machinery and so on.

In the early years after the revolution the optimism it had generated swept most Cubans along in the struggle against underdevelopment. They also received some immediate relief from the poverty in which they had been living, at least compared to what they had had to contend with before. The economist and Nobel Prize winner Wassily Leontief described the first two years after the fall of Batista as 'a wonderful revolutionary honeymoon'. The government's demand-oriented policies and increased buying power helped many people make ends meet.

However, the great downside to these policies was that they had the effect of reducing the proportion of Gross National Product being spent on investment. Reserves were quickly used up, unemployment was transformed into chronic underemployment and planning shortages mounted. The wrong kind of investment goods were bought; for example, expensive tractors instead of less costly agricultural equipment. The transport system stagnated.

The uniformed managers, unused to normal work rhythms, tended to emulate Guevara by working all hours of the night, and hid their lack of experience behind a wartime habit of making decisions spontaneously.

With central planning, the Cubans tried to transform their country's chaotic industries into a functioning command economy. On 11 March 1961 a Central Planning Commission or *Junta Central de Planificacion* (JUCEPLAN) was set up at ministerial level to coordinate economic policy and control what remained of the private sector. Instead though of bringing order to the economic confusion, JUCEPLAN grew into a 'bureaucratic monster' that more often than not tended to disrupt the operation of the economy.

The flow of information from the bottom up, from enterprises to the planning authorities and ministries, would get lost somewhere in the 'labyrinth of papers'; while directives from above, not infrequently bearing little relation to reality, often never reached the factory floor. JUCEPLAN was 'not fulfilling its managerial task of directing', as Guevara himself realised. In the autumn of 1960, Leo Huberman and Paul M Sweezy passed a somewhat more drastic judgement on the chronic disorder in economic planning; 'Chaos is perhaps too strong a word to describe the situation in his area, but it isn't all that far off it.'[188]

Almost miraculously, despite all the mistakes and all the disorganisation, in 1961 the economy still grew. The severe economic crisis that followed in 1962-63 forced the guerrillas standing at the levers of economic power to reconsider their policies. When the 'master of the Cuban economy', as one of his biographies called him, disappeared from the island's political scene in 1965, the legacy he left behind was clear to all; his eccentric 'guerrilla economy' had been more concerned with pursuing an ideological purism than with responding to Cubans' everyday needs. In stark contrast to the revolutionary slogans that had promised steady economic growth, production levels on the 'red island' were lower than they had been in Batista's time. Despite all the heroic effort that Guevara inspired in the production of sugar, not even this sector was able to overtake Batista's government economically. In 1962 the Cubans produced 4.8 million tonnes of sugar – about 700,000 tonnes less than in 1958.

The planning debate

It wasn't long before the heads of the command economy, and the Industry Minister especially, were coming under heavy criticism; Guevara had to take his part of the responsibility for the expensive and ill-fated plan to 'accelerate industrialisation'.

At the end of 1962 and the beginning of 1963 the voices of criticism were growing louder; they weren't only directed at him, but he remained their main target in so far he was the one principally responsible for the excessive centralisation of the Cuban economy and its overemphasis on industrialisation. After Castro had declared the socialist character of the revolution, questions of economic theory became a matter of urgent debate; in the summer of 1963 Guevara, as Minister for Industry, organised a discussion between the Minister for Foreign Trade Alberto Mora, the Finance Minister Luis Alvarez Rom, the President of the National Bank Marcelo Fernández Font, and the Marxist economists Charles Bettelheim from Paris and Ernest Mandel from Brussels. It was conducted as a series of articles in the journals *Nueva Industria* and *Comercio Exterior*.

Reduced to its simplest terms, the principal question in what was to become known as the 'planning debate' was which economic factor was best capable of regulating the production process. It could no longer be the market; its status as an basic element of capitalism ruled it out. But neither could it yet be human needs, because the material conditions for this were still lacking. So the participants in the debate created a sort of economic mutant; it was 'market' planning that should determine what should be produced, as well as when, where, and in what quantity. For Ernest Mandel, there existed a 'tertium datur beyond the dead ends of the market on the one hand, and the bureaucratic planned economy on the other'.

Together with the economist Charles Bettelheim, Mora emphasised the fact that the legal and the economic appropriation of formerly private means of production were two different things. Once the state had appropriated this property in a single political and legal act, the rest of society would still have to gain control over it, and the process would be complex and protracted because achieving that goal required a much higher level of development of productive forces than existed in Cuba. Mora claimed that 'state property is not yet the fully developed social property that will be attained only with Communism.'[190]

He suggested that this stage could be crossed by means of a system of 'financial self-management', according to which enterprises would not be made wholly subject to the socialised economy's central plan but would continue to enjoy a certain degree of autonomy. They would finance themselves through bank credits and manage their affairs on the principle of profitability, allowing banks a degree of control over those enterprises in debt to them. Exchange between enterprises would take place on a commercial basis, and they would have the freedom to encourage their workers' performance with material incentives such as production bonuses and piecework.

As the 'general manager' of the first years, Guevara's political convictions made him much more uncompromising. He argued for the 'budgetary finance system' that he'd instituted in the Ministry for Industry. According to it, the whole publicly-owned economy should be financed by the state budget and subject to the central plan; this meant specifically rejecting material incentives as a means of increasing production.

The crucial question in this debate was what role the law of value would, and indeed should, play as 'regulator of production' during the transition period to a socialist society. The controversy centred on two alternatives: either to accept things as they were and continue to tolerate the law of value, or to go over to the 'principle of conscious planning'; in other words, to abolish the law of value as soon as possible. For Guevara, chief planner and leading ideologue, who would have dearly loved to make categories like 'commodity' and 'money' disappear, the answer was clear;

Song in honour of Fidel

When you demand with ringing
   voice:
Land reform, justice, bread and
   freedom!
We shall be at your side with
   the same demand.

And when the beast is licking
   its wounds
Where the lance of national
   liberation has pierced it,
We shall with all our hearts be
   at your side.
   Ernesto Che Guevara, July 1955

Thus we can say that centralised planning is the essence of socialist society, is the category by which it is defined, and is the point at which human consciousness finally succeeds in taking control of the economy and directing it towards its goal of the complete liberation of human beings within Communist society.[191]

Instead of Adam Smith's 'invisible hand', which regulated the production process behind the backs of [its] economic subjects, Guevara wanted to see a plan instituted that was consciously designed to meet the needs of human beings. Ultimately he conceived of planning as the means by which socialist society would be led into the realm of freedom.[192]

Thanks to it, we will be able to approach the ideal of a direct economy by means of mathematical analyses, determining the correct distribution of resources between accumulation and consumption, and between the different branches of production, while never forgetting that human nature, the raison d'etre of our revolution and of our efforts, cannot be reduced to a mere formula.[193] This was the essence of Guevara's position in the debate.

Che's ideological purism and rhetorical brilliance, not to mention his reputation as brain of the revolution, meant that he had a very powerful influence on the so-called planning debate; but his model was never adopted on a wider front. Both models, the systems of 'financial self-management' and of 'budgetary financing' have in fact more or less 'peacefully coexisted' among different sectors of the Cuban economy. To this day, Cuban economic policy has swung back and forth erratically between the two models. At times it has tended towards Guevarism; then 'real socialist' emphases would reassert themselves, and it would swing the other way. The consequences for the development of the Cuban economy have been disastrous.

History of failure

The theory of guerrilla war

In the speech he delivered in memory of his former comrade, Castro paid homage to Guevara both as 'a remarkable champion of our revolution'[194] and as a 'virtuoso of guerrilla war', both as a 'man of action' and as a 'profound thinker'. Guevara's achievements did indeed go beyond the military talents and heroism he showed during the war of liberation; for he used his experiences from this conflict, together with historical analogies, to formulate a theory of guerrilla war.

Like many other theorists of the international workers' movement, Guevara based his ideas on warfare on the work of the famous military strategist, Carl von Clausewitz. The influence of Clausewitz's legendary work *On War* is very clear in Guevara's *Tactics and Strategy in the Latin American Revolution*; here for example is how he summarises its thesis: *Tactics and strategy are two essential elements of the art of war, but war and politics are closely related to each other by a common purpose, by the task of achieving a given aim, which is to destroy of the enemy in armed struggle and seize political power.*[195] The influence of a number of pioneers of guerrilla war can be found in Guevara's thoughts on this subject, including, among others, Mao Tse Tung, Simón Bolívar and the heroes of the Mexican revolution.

A major source of inspiration was undoubtedly the career of Augusto César Sandino, the 'General of the Oppressed', who from 1927 to 1933 had kept the American forces of occupation in Nicaragua tied down for five long years in what was the first modern guerrilla war, eventually forcing them to withdraw from the Central American isthmus.[196]

However, Guevara drew most of his lessons from the Cuban war of liberation. Time and again he specifically emphasises that *all the methods we have worked out here* were based on the experiences of the Cuban people's *war of liberation*.[197]

He had also urgently warned against dogmatically applying these experiences to other potential arenas of guerrilla war; yet this was precisely the error he himself would commit in Bolivia.

Guevara believed that three fundamental lessons could be drawn from the events of the Cuban war of liberation:

1. Popular forces can win in a war against a regular army;

2. It is not always necessary to wait until all the conditions for a revolution have matured: the uprising itself can itself create such conditions;

3. In the underdeveloped countries of the Latin American continent the struggle must principally be carried out in the countryside.[198]

This was precisely what the 26 July Movement demonstrated: that it was possible not only to challenge a powerful regular army with a group of very determined men – as had happened with the storming of the Moncada barracks in Santiago de Cuba – but also to defeat it.

Anyone unwilling to wait until circumstances had become at least partially favourable for revolution could have no moral reservations about armed conflict. Guevara admitted he had no qualms about using violence, which he characterised as *the midwife of the new societies*.[199] Anyone supporting the revolution had to accept its consequences, and since – as far as he was concerned – class struggle was unavoidable, it followed that *We should not fear violence, which is the midwife of the new societies; we should be concerned only that it is unleashed at a time when the peoples' leaders have determined circumstances to be favourable.*[200]

In contrast to orthodox Communists, for whom the cities represented the main revolutionary arena, for Che it was the countryside. This recommended itself as a field of action precisely because most Latin American countries were predominantly rural societies whose population lived off the land, the only exception being Argentina. The struggle that would be conducted from these regions would be an agrarian revolution, but as it spread from the hinterlands to the cities it would also radicalise; that is to say, it would grow into a socialist revolution. Working together with revolutionary forces in the cities, the guerrillas would operate from a 'fortress in the countryside'. Put simply, Guevara's main idea was to *surround the cities* from the countryside.[201]

The fact that peasant farmers and labourers were one of the most oppressed and exploited sections of the population under the existing regime also spoke in favour of a guerrilla war in the country. As such, they constituted the greatest reservoir of possible recruits to the people's army that the guerrilla movement would eventually become – an army capable of challenging the regular armed forces.

The other advantage of a guerrilla war was that the liberation fighters could seek or avoid confrontation with government troops as and when it suited them. Using the hit and run tactics that had been practiced by Sandino with increasing success, the guerrillas could attack army units from nowhere and then disappear again before the enemy was ready to counterattack. *Biting and running* was Guevara's term for this; *Biting, retreating, waiting, laying an ambush, attacking again and retreating once more; making sure the enemy never has a moment's peace.*[202]

'Guerrilla' means literally 'little war', although given the word's importance in Guevara's theories its diminutive form is somewhat misleading. He defined guerrilla war as *irregular armed struggle against enemies with potentially overwhelming military power.*[203] The conflict would begin with the celebrated *foco* conducting a 'little war' in the country's hinterland, inflicting a series of military 'pinpricks' on the armed forces; then would then draw in revolutionary sympathisers and gradually grow into a popular mass movement. This was precisely why Guevara could be certain that *guerrilla war is a people's war, is a struggle by the masses. To attempt to prosecute this kind of war without the support of the population is the prelude to inevitable catastrophe.*[204] We shall probably never know why in Bolivia in 1967 he ignored this insight and attempted to conduct a guerrilla war without the support of rural population.

The African dream

Che Guevara might not have become the revered revolutionary idol he did had he been satisfied with his part in just one, namely the Cuban, revolution. Instead of contenting himself with this and indulging in reminiscences of the Cuban war of liberation, he let his thoughts to travel far beyond Cuba's coasts to new shores. He had hopes of bringing about radical political change in his own country of Argentina, and, as one would expect of a declared internationalist and pan-American, he dreamed of a *revolution across the entire continent*. Following his years of political apprenticeship in Guatemala, he had become convinced that this region would one day become one of the most important arenas of revolutionary struggle.

However, the daring attempt to 'export' the revolution to Nicaragua, Panama and the Dominican Republic immediately after the rebels entered Havana in 1959 failed miserably. Five years later, in 1964, Guevara's thinking on this had changed. He gave the strategy of exporting the revolution a new turn when he came to conceive of the 'Dark Continent' as a prime focus of world revolution. In an interview of December 1964 he described Africa as *one of the most important arenas, if not the most important, in the struggle against every form of exploitation in the world, in the struggle against imperialism, colonialism and neo-colonialism.*[205] He reiterated this belief in a speech he gave on 12 February 1965 in the Tanzanian capital Dar-es-Salaam; *I am convinced that it is possible to create a common front against colonialism, imperialism and neo-colonialism.*[206]

A *common front* meant a tri-continental movement that would fight for the independence of peripheral countries in Asia, Africa and Latin America; hence his slogan *create two, three {...} many Vietnams*.

By joining the struggle against neocolonialism in the Congo, 'the eternal heart of darkness',[207] he hoped to relieve the revolutionary front elsewhere – namely Vietnam – and thereby help the liberation fighters in that country. Guevara calculated that as conflicts in other regions forced the United States to reduce its military presence in South-East Asia the chances of a Vietcong victory would increase.

As the Algerian statesman Ben Bella later recalled, Guevara had become convinced that *Africa was the one continent in the world most ripe for great changes; Africa set the course for the renewal of anti-imperialist struggle*.[208] Perhaps its was the rapid progress of decolonisation that had led Guevara to this astonishing conclusion; perhaps, too, it was an expression of his notorious optimism. Whatever the case, he needed a justification for his 'intervention' in Africa; for he was planning to use the so-called liberated territories there as a training ground for guerrilla war in those Latin American countries where social relations did not yet seem mature enough for revolution.

From the end of 1964 to the beginning of 1965 he made an extended fact-finding mission through the capitals of the radical African states that were supporting the Congolese rebels, meeting, among others, the Egyptian President Gamal Abdel Nasser, to whom he quite candidly revealed that he and a group of black Cubans were going to fight for the rebels in the former Belgian Congo (the present-day Democratic Republic of the Congo). *I'm going to the Congo*, he explained, *because it's the most important conflict in the world today {...} I think that in Katanga we can strike a blow against the imperialists at the centre of their interests*.[209]

Nasser was shocked by Guevara's plan to place himself at the head of the rebellion against neo-colonialism in Central Africa.

He rather ironically warned him against becoming 'a second Tarzan, a white man alone among blacks', but this warning was meant seriously. Both Nasser and the Algerian head of state Ben Bella tried hard to persuade him not to go, but Guevara wouldn't let himself be deterred; later it would become evident that, by this time in his career, he probably saw few other alternatives for political activity. What Guevara described as the *African dream* has in fact gone down in history as just that: a dream; and as a *story of failure*.

Che's 'Cuban saga'[210] ended in December 1964; a few weeks later he embarked on his 'African odyssey'. He offered only cryptic explanations for his sudden departure; his farewell letter, written in March but not made public by Castro until October of that year,[211] claims that *Other peoples of the world are in need of my modest help*. This could only mean that he had decided to throw overboard the ballast of his political responsibilities and seek new scenes of revolutionary struggle, free from the burdens of office.

First, though, he travelled north into what José Martí called the 'belly of the monster' – the United States – where he set out Cuba's position *on the most important issues of controversy*.[212] On 11 December 1964 he delivered a furious speech before the 19th General Assembly of the United Nations, in which he spoke bitterly of *the terrible events in the Congo*. Casting diplomatic language aside, he denounced *the tragic role that the imperialists have forced the United Nations to play there*, and angrily rounded on Belgium and the United States. A few weeks earlier, Belgian parachutists and South African mercenaries had recaptured the provincial capital of Stanleyville from the rebels at the cost of several thousand lives.

All free people of the world must arm themselves, warned Guevara, *to avenge the crime being committed in the Congo*.[213] The 'troubles in the Congo' had begun after the Belgian colony had made its overhasty and ill-prepared transition to independence on 30 June 1960. The murder in January 1961 of Patrice Lumumba, the

Congo's first prime minister, reignited power struggles for the country's vast mineral wealth and focussed US interests on its geopolitical importance. Lumumba, whom many Congolese accorded an almost godlike status, was suspected by the USA and Belgium of being a Soviet protégé; he was overthrown and killed because he had opposed their plans for a post-colonial regime dominated by Western multinationals.

The men who had conspired against him were Joseph-Desiré Mobutu, who seized power after Lumumba's fall, and Moise Tshombe, who wanted the copper-rich province of Katanga to secede from the rest of the country. When fighting broke out again after UN troops withdrew on 30 June 1964, the Congolese president Joseph Kasavubu seized upon an unusual tactic: he made the secessionist Tshombe Minister-President of the whole country. In the meantime the rebellion that had begun in the west spread eastwards to Lake Tanganika, led by Lumumba's former aides.

With revolutionary haste, Guevara set himself at the head of the 'left-orientated' rebels against the 'pro-western' regime of Tshombe,[214] and clearly did so in the belief that he was preparing the ground for a pan-African revolution. Having made his denunciatory speech at the United Nations he didn't return to Cuba, but instead made a tour of Africa's potentially revolutionary states.

Between Christmas 1964 and February 1965 he visited Algeria, Mali, Congo-Brazzaville, Guinea, Ghana, Dahomey, Tanzania and Egypt, meeting such illustrious statesmen as Ben Bella, Kwame Nkrumah, Julius Nyerere and Gamal Abdel Nasser. He also made contact with representatives of the rebels, including, among others, Gaston Soumaliot, self-declared 'President of North-East Congo', and Christophe Gebenye, whose troops had captured Stanleyville. Of all the freedom fighters Guevara met while crossing the country, none impressed him so much as Laurent Kabila, then in his mid-twenties and already the commander of a considerable section of the rebel troops. Guevara found him easy to work with, and there seemed to be a basic agreement between the two. Later he singled him out for praise; *Kabila was perfectly clear that the main enemy was North American imperialism, and appeared to be determined to fight it resolutely to the end. As I said, I was much impressed by his words and his apparent determination.*[215]

Guevara would be forced to drastically revise this impression in the course of his African campaign. It was still a while, though, before the Argentinian would join the battle on the side of the 'freedom fighters'. He returned to Cuba on 14 March, and on his arrival the simmering conflict with Castro took a decisive turn for the worse. Relations between the two men had almost completely broken down, and their differences seemed irreconcilable.

Che landed back at Ranchos Boyeros airport from a journey that had taken him across the world, including Beijing, and when he first got off the plane all the customary protocol seemed in place. Castro, his brother Raúl, and President Osvaldo Dorticós

Guevara receives a dressing down from Castro on his return to Havana on 14 March 1965. President Osvaldo Dorticos (centre) looks on disapprovingly

Guevara delivers a report on his African journey

had arrived to welcome him with the usual ceremony. But what happened next gave some indication of the changed political climate that awaited him. The customary press conference was not held, nor was the road from the airport lined by any cheering crowds. Instead, there were grave discussions behind closed doors. Every one of Che's possible political 'offences' were brought up; his flirtation with Beijing, his digs at the economic systems of the 'fraternal' socialist countries, his polemics against Cuba's Communist old guard and his personal criticism of Castro. Above all, though, there was the withering attack he had made on the Soviet Union in Algeria in February 1965, where he had delivered a speech at an economic seminar of the Afro-Asian Solidarity Conference. In it, he had openly accused the socialist countries that were taking advantage of the terms of trade with third world countries – namely high world market prices for manufactured goods and low ones for raw materials – of being complicit in 'imperialist exploitation', categorically insisting that *the socialist countries have the moral duty to end their silent complicity with Western exploiter nations.*[216]

This was going too far. Such an affront to Cuba's ally and protector was unforgivable. Sooner or later, Castro would have to act to preserve Moscow's support for the revolution. It already spoke volumes that he let his brother Raúl itemise his list of sins with Guevara; in so doing, he was giving him the signal that it was time for him to leave the political stage in Cuba and seek another field of activity, namely in Africa and the Congo.[217] Fidel urged his Comandante Che to return to Africa and lead the Cuban guerrillas.[218]

One of the peculiar things about the Cuban revolution, what made it such an object of fascination for the Left both in Europe and the United States, was that it had at its head not one but two leaders. It was led not by a single charismatic comandante but by two, both of whom became revolutionary icons for students in Berlin, Paris, Stanford and elsewhere. Castro, the Number One, and Guevara, the Number Two, were in many respects similar, but what united them above all was a *romantic feeling for adventure*, as Che called it when recalling his first guerrilla training in Mexico with the Cuban rebel commander.

As long as the issues to be decided were military and Castro was the *comandante en jefe*, the two got along famously. But once the war was over and they had descended from the mountains, taken up the 'burdens of the plains' and embarked upon the radical transformation of Cuban society, disagreements between them began increasingly to emerge.

'Che's complete loyalty to Fidel was beyond doubt. But it was also known in higher government and party circles that Che was the only member of the political elite who dared challenge Fidel when he didn't share his views.'[219]

Given that Castro as a rule would tolerate no criticism or contradiction, this was considered outrageous impertinence. The situation became still more precarious when it became clear that in matters of theory, Che and not Castro was the Cuban revolution's 'Number One'.

A Puerto Rican proverb describes the situation that had arisen five years after the revolution; 'One cave is too small for two male crabs.'[220] One of the men had to go, and for all his intransigence it had to be Guevara. At the beginning of April 1965 he set off in pursuit of a new revolutionary challenge.

For all its ambition, the mission would prove to be profoundly misguided. On 2 April he left Havana in strict secrecy for Dar-es-Salaam. Che's guerrilla war in Africa became 'the best kept secret of the Cuban revolution',[221] his destination and

Che giving a speech at Havana's Magna Aula University, 1961

mission being known only among a handful of people at the top of government. Apart from these, only the Soviet ambassador Alexander Alexeyev was let into the secret. Exact details of the Congo mission only became known in 1994, when the chronicle of failure was published in Havana. The book, edited by the Cuban journalists Foilan Escobar and Felix Guerra, and the Mexican novelist Paco Ignacio Taibo II, was a compilation of interviews with survivors, historical documents and extracts from a text by Guevara based on his diaries which had never before been published; its revealing title was *Our Year in Limbo*.

Between 22 March, when he disappeared from public view, and 3 October 1965, when Castro read out his letter of farewell, there was wild speculation over what had happened to Guevara. How could there be a May Day parade without Che? How could he not show up for the sugar harvest? His absence from both was shocking, and grotesque rumours ran wild.

Some reports claimed that Guevara had been seen in Brazil, others that he had been killed fighting US Marines in the Dominican Republic. Still others had it that he was being treated for exhaustion in a Cuban sanatorium, that he had gone mad and was being held at a Mexican clinic, that he had been sent to Siberia by the Soviets, that he had become a monk and retired to Spain, or that he had been kidnapped by an anti-Castro group and was being held in the USA. It was even rumoured that Fidel had had him shot.

When at press conference on 30 April the '*maximo lider*' encountered a barrage of such questions, he replied with the vague statement that, 'All I can tell you about Comandante Guevara is that he is always where the revolution most needs him.'[222] This meant in effect, everywhere and nowhere.

He had indeed taken leave of his companions, what he called *a bittersweet duty*.[223] But he had not done so without first leaving behind a letter for Castro to make public to the Cubans when the time came. In it he formally resigned from all his posts in the Party leadership, his job as minister, his rank of commandant, and, not least, his Cuban citizenship. *I am no longer bound to Cuba by any law.*

He renounced his second homeland in order to carry on his political mission in other destinations of the so-called Third World. *I can do what your responsibilities as leader of the revolution in Cuba prevent you from doing. The time has therefore come for us to part. You should know that I do feeling both joy and sorrow. I am leaving behind my greatest hopes for a better society, and I am leaving the people I love most, a people that has adopted me as a son. That hurts me deeply. I take with me to new fronts the faith that you have taught me, the revolutionary spirit of my people, and the feeling that I am fulfilling the most sacred of all duties – of fighting imperialism, wherever it may be. That is something that can still the deepest pain.*[224]

A month after he disappeared from Havana he arrived in Dar-es-Salaam, capital of the new republic of Tanzania. Together with a dozen veteran guerrillas, he made his way west to Kigoma on Lake Tanganika, where the rebel forces had their 'billets'. From here they crossed the lake and headed for the Congolese village of Kibamba, which the rebels had designated a 'liberated territory'.

More Cubans arrived over the next few weeks, altogether more than a hundred; their job was to help train the rebels in guerrilla warfare and if absolutely necessary fight alongside them. Cubans were still arriving in Kibamba at the beginning of September, when it had been clear for some time that the Congo mission was failing. Guevara and his men were paying the price for the ill thought-out revolutionary enthusiasm with which they had embarked on the Congo adventure, an enthusiasm that paid scant regard to the region's complex ethnic, cultural and political situation.

He frankly admits at the beginning of his diary that *this is a story of failure*; a failure in every respect – human, political and not least of all military. At a meeting with the rebels he had spoken about his experiences in the war of liberation and drawn conclusions from them on how to train the Congolese fighters; their reaction was extremely frosty. Guevara had evidently underestimated his partners' determination to do things their own way.

They felt they didn't need an outsider, and a white man at that, telling them how to fight their own war, and certainly not one possessed of such insufferable revolutionary zeal. They preferred their own more leisurely way of doing things. Guevara soon realised that the upper ranks were regularly *appallingly drunk*, and had no intention – indeed were incapable – of making any military advances.

Little by little Che's opinion of Kabila changed. He spent most of his time in the cities, principally Cairo; frequently he would send word that he was on his way to the front, only to call or telegram again with some excuse for why he was unable to return to the field of operations.

In Guevara's diary, a sort of war report supplemented by

analyses, disparaging remarks about Kabila's absence become increasingly frequent. *Every morning it's the same story: Kabila won't be coming today, but he will tomorrow or definitely the day after tomorrow.* While the Cubans accepted the hardships of the guerrilla war more or less stoically, its leader was living in comfort hundreds of miles away from *this Godforsaken place.* Guevara noted bitterly that *he lets days go by without thinking of anything other than political squabbles. And from everything I hear he's too fond of drink and women.*[225]

He soon came to the depressing realisation that *the Congolese revolution* was *destined to fail as a result of its own weaknesses.*[226] By the time Che, operating under the pseudonym 'Tatu', arrived in the theatre of operations, the revolution was already ending before it had properly begun. 'We got to the Congo too late,' was how the Algerian Ben Bella summed up his own involvement; the same is true for Guevara and the hundred or so Cubans who got there still later. By that time, the pathetic troop of African 'freedom fighters' was already in process of disintegration.

From the very beginning Che was being *constantly struck by one thing: lack of organisation.* This complaint would never go away,

Che, alias Tatu, teaching Guerrilla warfare in the Congo, 1965

and eventually led him to conclude that *it causes chaos to get into everything, and with increasingly manic enthusiasm.*[227]

That wasn't his only criticism of the Congolese troops; among other things, he found fault in their low fighting morale, lack of discipline, reluctance to make sacrifices and their tendency to live parasitically off the local population.

There was, for example, superstition; some soldiers believed that a magical drink called 'dawa' would make them invincible in battle. His analysis of all these faults is so unyielding that one senses in it not only a degree of arrogance but also certain racist undertones. What he'd hoped would be a heroic struggle was descending into farce, and as it did so Guevara himself reveals how cutting he would eventually become about his companions' failings when he notes disparagingly that the Congolese couldn't hit a cow at five metres. *The Cubans have to do everything* – this bitter reproach was the beginning of the end of the 'African dream'.[228]

On 20 June a force of forty Cubans, together with Congolese rebels and Tutsi soldiers, prepared an attack on some barracks and a power station in the town of Bendera. When it came to the battle, most of the Tutsis turned and fled while the Congolese soldiers went on strike, refusing to fire a single shot and leaving the Cubans to carry out the mission by themselves. They lost four men, all of whom had been carrying personal papers with them, in explicit contravention of orders. This was hard proof of Cuba's involvement with the rebels in the Congo, and the Tshombe regime was able to present it triumphantly to the world.[229]

Towards the end of July the rebels, with Cuban help, succeeded in luring government soldiers into an ambush; by the end of October, however, they had suffered another bitter defeat near Baraka. In the meantime discontent had spread among the Cubans. They resented having to risk their lives for what was a caricature of a rebellion. Back at their camp they had enormous supplies of arms at their disposal, but in the field they saw repeatedly and with mounting fury how well-armed rebels would throw away their rifles in panic at the first shot and run off into the undergrowth.

At the end of September Guevara admitted that; *Our situation was getting worse and worse.* After much soul-searching he came to the actually rather obvious realisation that *we can't liberate a country that doesn't want to fight {...}.* After all his bitter experiences, he still thought of it as *the so-called Congolese revolution.* When the Confederation of African States called on its members 'not to involve themselves in the internal affairs of other countries', this was for Guevara *the coup de grace to the doomed revolution.* After all their defeats, the rebels' morale was at its lowest ebb. In the Cuban camp there was simmering discontent, and many wanted to go home sooner rather than later.

White mercenaries from South Africa and Rhodesia in the service of Tshombe's regime, and under the command of the notorious Major 'Mad Mike' Hoare, were closing in their positions. Che's state of health was also deteriorating. It was time to retreat, and with Castro's help the Cubans were able to withdraw. Guevara later summed things up: *during our last hours in the Congo I felt more completely alone than I have ever done, either in Cuba or anywhere else.* It is painful to see what difficulty he had in finding anything positive to say about the fiasco that was the Congo expedition, so as not to have to return to Cuba completely disillusioned; *Victory is an important source of positive experiences*, he wrote, *but the same is true of defeat.*[230]

The Bolivian tragedy

The 'permanent revolutionary' spent three gloomy months in Tanzania and another few weeks, from the end of February to the beginning of March 1965, in Prague, before returning to Havana in the strictest secrecy. He was already preparing another revolutionary undertaking, this time in the centre of Latin America; although exactly where a revolutionary *foco* should be formed was still an open question. Peru seems to have been his first choice, and in mid-1966 Che was still only thinking of Bolivia as a staging post for a guerrilla war in Peru;[231] eventually, however, he decided on Bolivia as the most suitable place to begin a guerrilla war.

In retrospect the choice seems a strange one. In 1963 Castro himself had told Mario Monje, the General Secretary of the Bolivian Communist Party, that it would be very difficult to fight a guerrilla war in Bolivia for the simple reasons that the country was land-locked and had already undergone a land reform. A year later Guevara had taken the same position, *I've been to Bolivia*, he argued, *I know Bolivia, and it's very difficult to conduct a guerrilla war there. The country has already had a land reform, and I don't think that the Indians would join a guerrilla war.*[232]

Those were his words; yet two years later this was precisely what he was trying to do. It was the most astonishing blunder, for almost all the necessary conditions for a successful war were lacking. Had Che done at least some proper preparation for his operations in Bolivia, he could scarcely have overlooked how unsuited the country was for them, both socially and politically. United against external intervention in a nationalist consensus, political forces from left to right kept well away from Guevara.

Even the Bolivian Communist Party gave him the cold shoulder; indeed, they did everything they could to make things difficult for Guevara.[233] The Soviet Union did not approve of Che's activities in Bolivia, and in this case the officials of the Bolivian Communist Party faithfully

He was a man who had dedicated himself to an idea – a true utopian. He genuinely believed that he could create a better world; and I suspect [...] he was disillusioned by what was happening in Cuba. He tried to start again in the Congo, but that also didn't work. Then he tried going to Bolivia and starting again there, but Utopia kept slipping further and further away. When you reach for Utopia it always slips further away, further and further.

Dolores Moyano

followed the Kremlin's line. To them Guevara was nothing more than an adventurer indulging his own anarchic romanticism.[234] As a result the operation lacked what it urgently needed according to Che's own theory, namely centres of support in the city.

In the countryside things seemed no better. Instead of moving like fish through water, the guerrillas found themselves stranded high and dry. Their revolutionary zeal met with a wall of indifference and enmity; rather than joining the guerrillas the peasants even formed a front against them, and on occasion betrayed their movements to the Bolivian army. Despite all the efforts of Guevara and his comrades to gain their trust, they didn't manage to recruit a single peasant for their pitiful 'army of liberation'.[235] In the course of the war Guevara would note with astonishment that *an absolute silence reigned {in the villages}, as if we had found ourselves in another world*.[236] It was indeed another world. Bolivia was not Cuba; the Indians in the countryside had little in common with the peasants of the Sierra Maestra, and the political situation was hardly comparable with what had existed under the Batista dictatorship.

General René Barrientos, who in November 1964 had overthrown President Paz Estenssoro in a classic Latin American military coup, did everything he could to nip any kind of political opposition in the bud, while simultaneously building a formidable support base among rural workers. The arrogant new US-backed dictator was so successful at this that he could risk calling a presidential election only a year and a half later. It was held on 6 July 1966 and won him a resounding 62 per cent of the vote. This was the situation awaiting Che when he arrived in Bolivia.

In July 1966 Guevara had recently returned to Cuba. He spent a while recovering from his hardships in Africa in San Andrés de Taiguanabo at the foot of the Cordillera de los Organos, before planning his final expedition with renewed energy. Despite all the tensions with Raúl and Fidel, he was allowed to put together his own team; it included comrades who had been part of the

Self-portrait taken in Dar es Salaam, Tanzania, 1966

'invasion force' in western Cuba, others who had accompanied him to the Congo, and a few who had worked day and night with him at the Ministry of Industry trying to set up the 'guerrilla economy'.

Of the seventeen Cuban guerrillas who had immediately started training, four were members of the Central Committee of the Cuban Communist Party; among them was Jesús Suárez Gayol, deputy minister for industry and a trusted friend of Che's since the battle of Santa Clara. Five held the rank of *comandante*, one of the highest in Cuba's military hierarchy. Guevara explained to them, however, that officers' ranks would count for nothing in Bolivia; they would all fight there as simple soldiers, each under his own *nom de guerre*. Guevara's deputy in the Ministry for Industry, for example, became 'Rubio', Harry Villegas Tamayo, one of his most loyal comrades in arms, became 'Pombo', while Eliseo Reyes Rodriguez became 'Orlando'.[237] Only three of them would survive the war in Bolivia and make the difficult way back home through Chile, arriving in Cuba on 6 March 1968.

The Cuban guerrillas trained hard, going on forced marches in the mountains in the morning and attending lecture courses in the afternoon so that they would know something about Bolivia when they arrived there. Meanwhile other preparations were in hand; a number of Bolivians arrived on the island for training, while Pombo, Papi and Pachungo (Alberto Fernandez Montes de Oca, also known as Pacho) travelled secretly to Bolivia to make preparations for the war on the ground.

This work of reconnaissance and making contacts had to be carried out in the strictest secrecy. Unlike in Cuba, the men planning to 'liberate' Bolivia and possibly other Latin American countries were undertaking a subversive operation. They went into the field as conspirators; an approach that was at best questionable, and whose consequences for the revolution were far-reaching; for it meant that most Bolivians – excepting the few who had joined the ranks of Guevara's guerrillas – would consider its legitimacy doubtful from the start. For the Cubans, it was precisely this strategy that justified their mission.

In the meantime the ground had been sufficiently prepared in Bolivia for Guevara to think it time to begin the daring expedition. Ricardo, alias Papi, Mbili, Chincholín, Chinchu or Taco had done good work, having managed, among other things, to extract at least a half-hearted agreement from the Bolivian Communist Party that if it came to an emergency they would join the rebels' ranks; this in a country that had not one but four Moscow-aligned Communist parties.[238] The mineworkers' leader Moises Guevara, one of the pro-Chinese Communists, contributed several recruits to the guerrilla army.

The most striking figure in Che's 'army', though, was Tamara Bunke. Born in Buenos Aires in 1937, she grew up in the mainly Communist milieu of her German parents, first in Argentina and then, from 1952, in East Berlin. Trained as a 'scout', she was assigned to Guevara while he was staying in East Germany as part of a government delegation. It proved to be a momentous meeting. Tamara became Tania, and on Che's instructions moved to Bolivia in the summer of 1964. There she enrolled at the University of La Paz to study pharmacy, while in her spare time giving German lessons, pursuing cultural interests, and participating in the city's intellectual life, where she became known for the strength, if not the sophistication, of her convictions. It was here that she got to know Anita Heinrich, a young woman of German origin and secretary to the then Minister for Justice, Antonio Arguedas Mendieta. This was a stroke of luck for the Cubans, and provided them with a number of sources of information.[239]

In mid-1966 she married a twenty-five year old Bolivian man, giving her name as Laura Gutíerrez Bauer; after their honeymoon she surprised many of her friends by sending her husband off to study in Bulgaria. In fact, the marriage was nothing other than a skilful move, for it gave her Bolivian citizenship – an important requirement for carrying out Guevara's plan.

In the summer of 1966 this meant buying a farm that would act as a cover for the guerrilla base. In July Ricardo closed a deal with the landowner Remberto Villa; for 3,000 pesos, about $2,500, he acquired about 2,000 acres of land in Ñancahuazú, south eastern Bolivia, 140 miles south east of the bustling provincial city of Santa Cruz. The farm was remote enough to allow preparations for the conflict to be carried out undisturbed, but not so isolated that the guerrillas would be in danger of operating in a social vacuum.

Che assumed an almost perfect disguise to travel to field of operations. The dashing freedom fighter, who had been compared with Robin Hood and Garibaldi, transformed himself with the help of skilled make-up artists into a respectable travelling salesman; bald but for a few grey hairs, in a pair of thick spectacles and a cheap suit, his pudgy corpulence suggested a man who consoled himself for his business failures with expensive meals. The transformation was an astonishing one, and when it was over Che himself took a picture of himself in the mirror of his hotel room.

Guevara set off posing as Adolfo Mena González, a Uruguayan businessman, passport number 130748; he also had on him a second passport with the name Ramón Benítez Fernández. On 23 October he flew from Havana to Moscow, and from there went on to Prague, where he and his companion Pachungo boarded a train for Vienna. The next station on this circuitous journey, which the CIA was later to unravel, was Frankfurt-am-Main, where he bought the pocket calendar that would later become the 'Bolivian diary'. From Paris he went on via Madrid to Sao Paolo; finally, on 6 November, he arrived in Corumba, on the border between Brazil and Bolivia.

The revolutionary disguised as the bourgeois: Che as Adolfo Mena González. A self-portrait taken in the Hotel Copacabana on the day that he arrived in La Paz, November 1966

He and his companion Pachungo were met there by a reception committee composed of Papi, Renan, Montero and Jorge Vazquez Machicado Viana, alias Bigotes. The group drove to Cochabamba and La Paz in two jeeps. During the journey Bigotes, who had evidently been left in the dark about Che's identity in order to protect it for as long as possible, experienced an acute sense of *deja vu* sitting next to their strange travelling companion before suddenly realising who he was. Guevara seemed greatly to enjoy this incident.[240]

On 7 November Che and his 'quartermaster' arrived at the place where the *foco* of the Latin American revolution would be established, and on this day the *'comandante'*, rightly described as a 'compulsive diarist',[241] wrote his first entry. *A new stage has begun today*, he announced, and went on, *we arrived at La Finca at night.*

The journey went well. After we'd travelled through Cochabamba in disguise, Pachungo and I made contact and travelled for two days by jeep, using two vehicles. We stopped when we got near the Finca, so as not to waken the suspicions of the local landowner, who's been spreading rumours that we're using the farm to produce cocaine.[242]

The suspicious landowner was Ciro Algarañaz Leigue, former mayor of the oil town of Camiri and now the guerrillas' neighbour, who followed their comings and goings day and night. The guerrillas kept on good terms with Algarañaz by buying chickens, geese and pigs from him. They withdrew from his watchful gaze a couple of days after their arrival on 10 November, when they *decided to go into the bush and pitch a base camp.*[243]

In so doing, they were exposing themselves to all the rigours of the forest, and in particular to its monstrous plague of insects that came in every shape and form; yaguasas, jején and marigui, a blood-sucking yellow insect with enormous wings that left one's body covered in terrible sores, not to mention mosquitoes and ticks. On top of this, the forest was full of thorny plants that tore the guerrillas' skin. The one meagre comfort was that among the region's varied flora and fauna were edible plants such as *palmitos* – palm hearts – and some reasonably palatable game, including monkeys, iguanas, parrots, wild turkeys, pigeons and visnas, a variety of small, black bird.

In the beginning their rations were plentiful and good. For breakfast there was coffee, milk and bread, as well as a small quantity of butter, for lunch rice, meat and beans, in the afternoon there was coffee and in the evenings again 'a hearty meal followed by more coffee'.[244] But by the end of February Guevara had to admit that *the last few days of hunger have shown how low our spirits have fallen*. From then on, hunger was a constant companion. On 4 March Guevara noted that *the mood among the others is bad and they are getting physically weaker every day; oedemas have appeared on my legs for the first time.*[245] In the beginning the guerrillas were still eager for action, visiting the field of operations in pairs in order not to arouse attention. They built a 'cabaña', a living quarters with tables and benches inside it, a clay oven in which to bake bread, a 'pharmacy', a 'library', and an entire system of tunnels and caves in which they stored documents, weapons and provisions.

But it was a liberation army that was still only made up of a handful of men. On 20 November the first four guerrillas were joined by 'Marcos', Antonio Sanchez Díaz, *comandante* and member of the Central Committee of the Cuban Communist Party, and 'Rolando', Captain Eliseo Reyes Rodríguez. On 27 November, three weeks after Che's arrival, another four Cubans arrived, all of them veteran guerrilla fighters, and for the first time two Bolivian 'recruits' found their way to the base camp from Ñancahuazú, to Che's great relief. He proudly noted that *now there are twelve of us*.[246] In December the guerrilla company grew to 24, only nine of whom were Bolivians. At the end of March 1967 the army of liberation reached its maximum strength of 46 fighters; in addition there was Tania, who was not a trained fighter, and four others who served only as porters. Altogether 49 men and one woman, Tania, were assigned to Che's command during the eleven months of the Bolivian campaign; 17 Cubans, 29 Bolivians, three Peruvians and one German.[247] Che seemed to have feared such an 'internationalisation' of the guerrillas for some time. The more foreigners joining the guerrillas in southeast Bolivia, the easier it became for others to discredit the liberation struggle as a foreign intervention. After the guerrillas' first successful attack on the Bolivian army, President Barrientos called on the nation to 'join the struggle against foreign and local anarchists who are being armed and supported by Castro's Communists'.[248]

By then Guevara could be glad that the Bolivians finally made up the majority, at least superficially, and were giving their force the appearance of the proper political make up. In reality, though, the Cubans set the tone; their predominance is evident in the almost tragi-comic allocation of duties that Guevara carried out on 12 December 1966. After lecturing his soldiers on the theme of discipline, *I then handed out appointments: Joaquin as acting military commander, Rolando and Inti as commissars, Alejandro as head of operations, Pombo responsible for transport, Inti for finances, Nato for supplies and arms, and Moro provisionally in charge of medical care.*[249] If one includes Che himself as commander-in-chief, then the group's leadership was made up of six Cubans and just two Bolivians.

In the Ñancahuazú camp in Bolivia. Hunger was a constant companion

What Guevara had confidently assumed would happen simply did not; the local peasants showed not the slightest intention of joining the army of liberation; rather the contrary; the foreigners' presence made them nervous and not infrequently *very afraid*. Over the entire course of their campaign the guerrillas didn't succeed in winning over a single peasant.

Their encounters with the Communists in La Paz were equally discouraging. Immediately after his arrival in Ñancahuazú, Che had again declared that *we must try to persuade the Party to fight*.[250] Days went by, however, without anything happening; *Nothing new from La Paz*, Che wrote in his diary on 18 and 19 November. The moment of truth didn't come until New Year's Eve, 1966.

Mario Monje Molina, head of the Bolivian Communist Party, arrived at the rebel camp at first light on the morning of 31 December accompanied by Tania, who had been instructed to bring him. Negotiations between these two very different Communists were tough, and ended abruptly after Monje let the cat out of the bag by claiming political and military leadership of the revolution for as long as it was taking place on Bolivian territory.

For Guevara this was utterly out of the question. He categorically stated that *I shall be the military commander-in-chief and shall accept no ambiguities about that {...} We left it at that so he could think it over and talk to the Bolivian companeros. We went on to another camp and he spoke to everyone there, putting the alternatives before them: they could either stay or they could support the Party. All of them stayed, and it seemed to me this made a big impression on him.*[251]

At midnight the two adversaries toasted the *continental revolution*; a few hours later Monje informed the guerrillas that he felt his job was done. *He walked like someone being led to the gallows* was how Che described Monje's departure[252] – evidently unaware of how dangerously complacent he was being. The same complacency is evident in his *Analysis of the Month* for January 1967, where he writes confidently that *The Party is now arming itself against us. I don't know how far they're ready to take things, but it isn't going to slow us down and in the long run it will be to the good (I'm almost certain of that). The most honest and militant people will side with us, even if they have to suffer a difficult crisis of conscience.*[253]

During lulls in the fighting Guevara would teach the guerrillas Quechua or give lessons on various theoretical subjects; on 12 April 1967, for example, he began *a short course on Debray's book.*[254] The book in question was *Revolution in the Revolution?*; published a few months earlier in Havana, it was already creating a furore among the Latin American Left. In 1963 the French writer Régis Debray had travelled around Bolivia on behalf of several Maoist groups. 'Castro had now sent him back with a rather different task. He was to examine and report on which part of the country was best suited to establishing a *foco*.'[255] He was also to provide help for Guevara's Bolivian operation.

Debray did not only act as a go-between for Fidel and Che, he was also a sort of spokesman for the two revolutionaries. Indeed, his book had been based on interviews with Castro and a selection of articles and speeches by Guevara, as well as his own observations; its thesis was that the guerrilla *foco* in the countryside represented the avant-garde of revolutionary struggle.[256]

At the end of February 1967 the Argentinian painter Ciro Bustos, Che's man in Argentina, flew to La Paz, where he had been instructed to take a bus to Sucre. Having boarded the bus he was surprised to notice a European among the passengers; this, he would soon discover, was Régis Debray. A short while later the bus was overtaken by a taxi which forced it to stop. A young woman got on; Tania, the *guerillera*. Bustos was horrified, for the incident broke all the rules of undercover operations. Three foreigners who appeared not to know each other were travelling together on the same bus to an area where foreign guerrillas were known to be active.

When the three of them reached Ñancahuazú, Guevara was still away on a reconnaissance patrol with his fighters. He returned a few days later, in time to restore the deteriorating discipline in the camp. Bustos was shocked by his appearance, 'He was a complete mess. His clothes were virtually falling off him; his shirt was hanging down in rags, his knees protruded from his trousers, and he looked genuinely emaciated. Despite all this he embraced me, and I was deeply moved; we did not speak.'[257]

And despite everything he was forging new plans that seemed to border on delusions of grandeur. He revealed to Bustos that *My strategic aim is to win political power in Argentina. I'd like to put a group of Argentinians together for this, I'd like to prepare a couple of columns, give them a year or two's combat experience fighting over here,*

then send them back to Argentina. You should take over this task.
Understandably, Bustos thought Che's plans unrealistic; 'It sounded somewhat magical, as if he didn't come from this world.'[258]

As if to confirm this impression, Che – who to outsiders had come to seem something of a physical and mental wreck – drafted a grandiose proclamation, *The National Liberation Army to the Bolivian People*, whose principal claim cast real doubt on whether the guerrilla leader was still in touch with reality; *The governing clique and their masters, the Yankee imperialists, are trembling before the mighty onslaught of our struggle {...} We shall not rest until the last trace of imperialist power has been eradicated, and the glorious people of Bolivia have achieved happiness, progress and prosperity.*[259]

There was no question of Tania now leaving the guerrillas' camp, for as Che noted on 27 March, *there's every indication that Tania has been singled out*[260] – in other words, her cover had been blown. There's some evidence that she'd given her identity away on purpose in order to change the role of undercover agent for that of guerrilla at Che's side. Given how experienced she was as an agent, it could hardly have been carelessness that caused her to behave so unprofessionally on her way to the guerrilla camp in Camiri. 'Although she had plenty of opportunities to leave her jeep at a friend's house [...], she parked it in the middle of town where everyone could see it, leaving all her personal effects inside. She counted on the fact that the jeep would inevitably come to the attention of the police. Only a few days earlier she had warned the Bolivian guerrilla Coco Peredo that the security forces had become suspicious as a result of the unusual comings and goings and the many new faces in the town; it could therefore have come as no surprise to Tania when she learned that police had confiscated the suspicious jeep a few days later.'[261]

Guevara it left up to Bustos and Debray how they would leave the camp; either under their own steam, or wait until the guerrillas carried out an operation in the neighbouring area and use the resulting confusion to escape unnoticed. Debray was even more eager than Bustos to return to civilisation, and Che's diary entry for 28 March shows that he thought Debray had lost his nerve; *The Frenchman*, he wrote, *keeps going on about how useful he'd be outside.*[262] As someone who feared no danger himself, Che was good enough to overlook this weakness. He gave Debray the task of making contact with the outside world by means of Communique No. 2, which he drafted himself, and by passing on a coded message to Castro. He also planned to give him letters to pass on to Bertrand Russell and Jean-Paul Sartre, in the hope of persuading them to start a fund-raising campaign for the Bolivian liberation movement.[263]

Some time later, when Guevara and his men were approaching Muyupampa, Bustos and Debray tried their luck. It proved to have run out; the Bolivian army had set up positions in the area and they ran straight into them. It was a hard blow for them but also a disaster for Guevara, who on 20 April noted tersely in his diary, *Things look bad for Carlos. Dantón should have got away, though.*[264] In his *Analysis of the Month* for April, he bemoaned the bitter loss that the capture of Bustos and Debray meant for the guerrillas' cause; *Dantón and Carlos were in too much of a hurry to get out of here; their haste bordered on desperation, and they fell victim both to it and to my own indecision over whether to stop them. The result is that our lines of communication with Cuba are now cut (Dantón), and our opportunities for dealing with Argentina are now lost (Carlos).*[265] Under interrogation, Bustos and Debray denied everything, Debray pretending to be a clueless French journalist. However, as the interrogation methods were made harsher he broke down and admitted that the guerrilla leader 'Ramón' was actually Guevara. Bustos had no choice but to confess as well. After the two of them had served almost three years of their 30-year prison sentence, they were freed and flown to Chile. Debray had won international fame at his trial and later became an adviser on

Latin America to the French President François Mitterand; he later subjected Castro and Guevara to bitter criticism, and disowned his former comrades.

Prelude to catastrophe

By now the guerrillas' nomadic existence had taken a series of disastrous turns. On 1 February Che had set off on a two-week reconnaissance mission with most of the guerrillas, 'but these two weeks turned into a harrowing forty-eight day ordeal, during which the troops lost their way and the men had to suffer hunger and thirst on their exhausting marathon marches.'[266] On top of this they had to deal with heavy rains, which caused the rivers to swell to raging torrents. While crossing one of these, two Bolivians were swept away and drowned. The guerrillas had lost two men before they had even seen any action.

Then on the way back to the camp Che and his followers came across increasing signs that the police and the army were on their trail. On 19 March Che noted his concern; *A light aircraft circled above us, which can mean nothing good.*[267] When he got back to the camp it was to news of the first desertions. Two Bolivians had run off, been captured by the Bolivian army and told them everything they knew about the guerrillas; Che was also told 'that the police had been to the Finca'. The army had discovered the guerrillas' hideout much earlier than expected, and too early for Guevara's plans. The element of surprise had been lost, and it was now the enemy, and not they, who had the initiative. 'Che's expedition never recovered from its ill-fated beginning. It staggered from one crisis to the next.'[268]

Hostilities, then, were opened before the ragged, starving and partly barefoot guerrillas were properly prepared for them. Occasionally they were able to take the initiative and entice the army into ambushes, as they did for the first time on 23 March, when they killed seven soldiers, wounded six others and took eleven prisoners, as well as capturing various rifles and machine guns with their ammunition. This was admittedly a victory, but it would soon prove a pyrrhic one; a 'prelude to catastrophe',[269] the beginning of the end of the mission.

On 28 April the commander of the United States' MILGP (Military Group) in Bolivia had signed a 'Memorandum of Understanding' with the commander-in-chief of the Bolivian armed forces with the aim of tracking down and destroying Guevara's guerrilla force. For this purpose they created a special Ranger Battalion, and from 'Southcom', the USA's southern command in Panama, known also as the 'School of the Dictators', a team of sixteen Green Berets were flown to Bolivia to train this 'second battalion' – a rapid attack force – in counter-insurgency operations. They evidently did a good job,[270] for it was Rangers from this unit who, at the beginning of October, finally brought a violent end to Che's dreams of starting a revolution in Bolivia that would spread across the whole of Latin America.

With his victories in Cuba behind him, Guevara had come to Bolivia hoping to repeat his successes; instead, he found himself up against a host of unexpected difficulties that made him ever more despondent and broke the guerrillas' morale. 'The army was on his trail; he had lost contact with Cuba, he had lost contact with the capital, La Paz. He couldn't get the peasants to cooperate. Many of them were sick. They lacked provisions. He was plagued by asthma. Morale had sunk. And on top of all this, the guerrilla force had split itself in two.'[271]

This was one of the most bizarre and tragic incidents of the whole operation – the division their already meagre force, which Che had named the '*Ejercito de Liberacion Nacional*' or 'National Liberation Army', into two groups. On 17 April, while Che was marching to Muyupampa with the main body of the force, he ordered the commander of the rear column, to whom he had assigned the less able-bodied fighters as well as the Bolivians that he considered unreliable, *to carry out some operations in the area so we*

Bolivian Rangers on the trail of the partisans

can avoid drawing attention to ourselves. He should wait for us for three days and then remain in the area, without engaging the enemy directly, and wait for us to return.[272]

Joaquín, the 'commander' of the ten-man rear column, faithfully followed his orders; despite this, Che's main column and its rear guard were never to find each other again. They scoured the forest in every direction searching for traces of the missing party, but the other group remained lost. More often than not, the guerrillas' poor-quality maps tended to lead them astray.

In his diaries, Che repeatedly bemoaned the predicament that was steadily undermining his men's morale. At the end of May 1967 he began his *Analysis of the Month* with the observation that *the real problem is that despite searching the mountains we still can't make contact with Joaquín.* At the end of June, he noted as his first *negative point {...} That we still can't make contact with Joaquín.* At the end of July he again lamented *not being able to make contact with Joaquín*, and at the end of August he yet again deplored the *lack of contact with Joaquín {...}.*[273]

By that time the rear column was no more. It had been wiped out on 31 August, leaving only one survivor; a coup for Captain Mario Vargas Salinas, whose orders had been to concentrate on destroying Joaquín's force. When Joaquín's group was sighted at the confluence of the Masicuri and the Rio Grande rivers, Vargas Salinas and his force of forty men struck camp and headed to intercept the guerrillas. Their guide was Honorato Rojas, a peasant farmer; in February, Che and some other guerrillas had visited his remote hut to buy provisions. On that occasion, Che had provided what medical assistance he could to both of Rojas' sons, one of whom was suffering from worms, while the other had been kicked by a horse.

At the end of August Rojas informed Captain Vargas Salinas that guerrillas were in the area; indeed, the Cuban guerrilla Alejandro had called on the farmer with several of his companions. They had asked him if he would take them to the ford the next day, where they believed Che and his column might be. Armed with this information, the Captain and his men set off. They marched all night so that they would get to Vado del Yeso, the place in question, by the next morning, and there they took up positions and waited for Joaquín and his men.

Crossing the Rio Grande

They waited all day; then late in the afternoon they started to make out some movements. The guerrillas appeared, with Tania visible among them. Hesitantly, constantly pausing as if wanting to make sure the coast was clear, they waded across the ford in single file. Once all of them were in sight, Vargas Salinas ordered his soldiers to fire at will. The soldiers fired for so long and so unrelentingly, even on the wounded who were being carried away by the river, that in the end only a single guerrilla was left alive.[274]

When he heard of what had happened Guevara simply would not believe it. He vehemently refused to accept what was happening to his operation, and treated news of this attack by the Bolivian army and its outcome as disinformation, aimed at demoralising his men. On 2 September he wrote *that the radio reported that ten men, led by a Cuban known as Joaqín, had been wiped out near Camiri. The report, however, was broadcast by the Voice of America; the local broadcasters mentioned nothing.*[275] The next day he was referring to the news of the fiasco at Vado del Yeso as a *deception tactic.* On 4 September he was still mocking the *curious news that is being spread about Masicuri and Camiri.*[276] It wasn't until 8 September, when the radio mentioned that President Barrientos had had Tania's body cremated and given a Christian burial, that he stopped trying to deny what had so clearly happened. Perhaps it was on this day that he accepted defeat was unavoidable; he had in any case only thirty days left to live.

The Bolivian expedition lasted for 335 days, and Che would have occasion to describe quite a few of them as *black.* There were, for example, the 23 and 25 February, the 25 April, the 26 June and the 14 August 1967. From the beginning of September, though, his mood noticeably darkened. The enthusiasm he'd shown in the early days was gone. The 29 August, a day on which two of the guerrillas had collapsed from lack of water, he found a *terrible and truly oppressive day*[277]. One entry in the diary dated 26 September begins tersely with the word *defeat.* He could no longer hide the fact that his 'army of liberation' was disintegrating. They had fallen into an ambush. Miguel, Coco and Julio had been killed, and Camba had *run off on the pretext of having left behind his backpack*. He had deserted, as had Leon.

The noose around Guevara was drawing ever tighter. On 11 April the Bolivian army had discovered the guerrillas' camp and found of photograph of him. The CIA were informed and promptly became active in Bolivia. Soon afterwards, Washington learnt from two deserters that Guevara was preparing a guerrilla war deep in the Bolivian countryside.

The same April the army went onto the offensive against the rebels. They deployed more than 2,000 soldiers against the tiny guerrilla army, supported and 'advised' by US instructors, experts in anti-guerrilla combat and CIA agents. A bounty of 50,000 pesos was offered for Che's capture, preferably alive. Finally, after about fourteen direct encounters or ambushes, and after 42 soldiers and 21 guerrillas had been killed, in late September the army of liberation found itself surrounded by the Bolivian military. By then, eight Cubans, seven Bolivians and two Peruvians were left alive in this calamitous war. After the Bolivian army's last attack and the executions that followed it, only three Cubans and two Bolivians survived. Except for the deserters who had left the guerrillas early on, the balance at the end was '94 dead and one immortal corpse.'[278]

What had all these sacrifices been for? In Che's third and last project, which he himself quite openly described as a *new adventure*, there is an unmistakeably suicidal streak. 'Our man', wrote one of his biographers, 'was not only fleeing contradiction; he was searching for his own tragedy.'[279] Driven by the 'blind optimism' that would be able to repeat the Cuban 'success story', he unwittingly led his comrades to their collective doom. Instead of self-critically setting his own limits, he ignored the awkward facts of reality, behaving as if in some deterministic sense he had been called to carry out a historic mission.

This myth, to which he greatly contributed himself, brought him an enthusiastic following. After the operation had ended in disaster, many of those who hadn't been among the select few that had gone to fight in Bolivia bitterly regretted they had not been able to follow Guevara to his death.

One of the striking things about the Bolivian adventure is that Guevara said almost nothing about the political plans he had for it. This was something that Debray noticed; 'As far as we knew, Che's real plans were never set down in writing, nor even made public. At no time did he explicitly or systematically set them out before the group of guerrillas in Ñancahuazú. The plans were ever-present, but they were treated as if they were self-evident and therefore in need of no proper formulation. Most people made guesses about what they were, others made assumptions; but only a few really knew.'[280]

By the first days of October, the guerrillas' final defeat was approaching. 'After six months the forlorn group was at the end of its tether; hunted by Indian Rangers who had been trained in North America, pursued by airplanes, betrayed by comrades who had been captured and tortured; with neither supplies nor a secure camp, they stumbled towards the end.'[281] Again and again Che complained that *we are isolated*. They no longer had a radio transmitter with which to contact Havana. At both the end of July and the end of August, Che noted a *total lack of contact*.[282] It almost seemed as if Castro had left the Cubans to their fate in Bolivia.

October 8, 1967 turned out to be the final disastrous day. The guerrilla force, or rather what was left of it, found itself surrounded in the Yuro ravine without any means of escape. 'Its stony slopes, culminating in bare mountain crags, are separated from each other by a series of small valleys, overgrown with dense forest, into which there flows a number of streams. It's a miserable place, utterly insignificant, and hundreds of miles from anywhere.'[283] Sixteen guerrillas faced a hundred soldiers; if they wanted to escape they would have to fight their way out. The battle began at ten minutes past one, and Che was hit by a round early in the afternoon. A severe asthma attack overcame him. Simón Cuba Sarabia, alias 'Willy', dragged the wounded man to the top of a slope, where they found themselves surrounded by several soldiers.

Captain Gary Prado Salmon was called over, and asked the guerrillas who they were, identifying the guerrilla leader by his heavy eyebrows and a scar. The impression made on him by Guevara stayed with him for the rest of his life. 'Che had a striking gaze, bright eyes, a mane of almost red hair and a longish beard. He wore a black beret, an absolutely filthy military uniform, a black hooded jacket, and his breast was almost completely bare because his shirt had lost all its buttons.'[284]

Prado first radioed the 8th Division's headquarters at Vallegrande at 2.50pm. 'Reports from the field claim capture of Ramón. We have not yet confirmed.' Half an hour later he was evidently no longer in doubt. 'Capture of Ramón confirmed', he radioed. In Vallegrande it was soon agreed that the General Staff in La Paz should be informed of the matter.

As darkness fell, Captain Prado and his valuable prize marched the two and a half kilometres back to La Higuera, a Godforsaken hamlet of 30 miserable huts and 500 inhabitants. After being bound hand and foot, Guevara was locked in the village school-house. Towards evening, Lieutenant-Colonel Andrés Selich asked the headquarters in Vallegrande what they were to do with Guevara, and received the order that they were to keep him in custody and await further instructions.

In La Paz, the government was uncertain exactly what to do with their world-famous prisoner. The storm of indignation that had descended from all over the world when they punished Debray so severely was still an unpleasant memory. Bolivia had no death penalty; consequently this far more famous prisoner would have to be kept in jail for many years to come, preferably in a high security prison (something they also didn't have). They would, they realised, be under constant threat of a Cuban commando unit trying to free him. As for sending the prisoner to the United States, there could be no question of that. Not only would such a solution be an insult the political and military authorities' national pride, it would provide exemplary proof of Che's claim that most Latin American countries were utterly subordinate to United States hegemony and interventionist policies.

Guevara himself was clearly convinced that the government in La Paz wouldn't dare execute him. *I'm worth more to you alive than*

Taken prisoner, Guevara allows himself to be photographed with the CIA agent Felix Rodriguez

dead, he is supposed to have told one of his guards.[285] He is also supposed to have said, *Don't worry, I'm sure that you are not going to have to keep me for long, since many countries will demand my release. There's no need for you to go to any trouble and you mustn't worry. I don't think anything's going to happen to me.*[286]

He was horribly wrong. The politicians and military commanders in La Paz preferred a quick and violent end for their prisoner to the protracted uncertainty of prolonged imprisonment. Without consulting the courts, but with the consent of President René Barrientos, they passed a sentence of death. At 12.30pm on 9 October the high command in La Paz radioed the order to eliminate 'Señor Guevara'.

It is not inconceivable that in so doing the Bolivian army was merely acting on the orders of the CIA. One version has it that 'after enquiries had been made in CIA headquarters in Washington and in the White House, the order came to murder Guevara [...]'.[287]

The former CIA agent Philip Agee, whose main area of operation from 1957 to 1968 was South America and who himself played a role in the operation against Guevara, has claimed several times that he was murdered on Washington's instructions. 'In October 1967 I was working undercover for the CIA as a diplomat in the American Embassy in Mexico City. I remember very well the people there congratulating themselves after Che had been captured and murdered. It was the outcome of more than ten years of attempts to "neutralise" Che.'[288] In other words, to kill him.

The American government had installed a five-man CIA task force in Bolivia, whose most important member was Félix Rodríguez, alias Félix Ramos; a Cuban-American who had extracted a large amount of information about Guevara's army of liberation from a captured guerrilla. The instructions he had received from CIA central command were unambiguous: 'do everything possible to capture him [Guevara] alive.' Despite this, it was he who conveyed the Bolivian high command's order to execute Guevara to the soldiers in La Higuera. He also took it upon himself to tell Che personally that he was about to be killed.[289]

Che's last words are supposed to have been, *Tell Fidel that this setback doesn't mean the end of the revolution; it will triumph elsewhere. Tell Aleida to forget me, marry again and be happy, and take care that the children work hard at school. And tell the soldiers to aim well.*[290]

That morning Major Miguel Ayoroa sought volunteers to carry out the sentence of death; Lieutenant Mario Terán, still visibly drunk from the victory celebrations of the day before, declared himself willing. According to him, three other Marios from his company had been killed by the guerrillas, and he wanted to avenge the deaths of his namesakes.

When the lieutenant entered the room where Che had spent his last eighteen hours, the Argentinian knew what was about to happen. He looked him straight in the eye and said *I know you've come here to kill me. Shoot, you coward, you're only killing a man.*[291] Terán hesitated. Then he put a dozen shots through Che's chest with his semi-automatic rifle; one of them went through his heart.

San Ernesto de La Higuera

Che Guevara died on 9 October 1967,[292] at the age of thirty-nine. In the afternoon his body was strapped to a helicopter and transported to Vallegrande. There it was washed and cleaned by four medical orderlies and two German nuns before being laid out on a concrete slab in a wash house behind the hospital of Nuestra Señora de Malta. With his head slightly raised, his eyes open and a curious smile around his lips, he looked as if he were still alive and about to engage his visitors in conversation. There were many of these on 10 October 1967. One by one, the peasants of Vallegrande filed past the body as it lay in state; they were followed by journalists from all over the world who would be persuaded that

Guevara had died in a skirmish near La Higuera. 'Latin America's formidable Christian tradition of worshipping wound-covered saints and tortured figures of Christ meant that Che's image was bound to have a powerful effect, evoking as it did death, salvation and resurrection [...]. That night, candles were lit in the small town's huts for the first time. A secular saint was born, a saint of the poor.'[293]

The nuns and the religious women of Vallegrande all agreed that the dead revolutionary bore an astonishing resemblance to Jesus. One after the other, they would come to take away a lock of hair as a relic. Today he is known among the Bolivian peasants as 'San Ernesto de la Higuera'. The day before, CIA agent Felix Rodriguez had asked Guevara whether he could take a photograph of him. Lending his Pentax to the helicopter pilot Major Nino de Guzmán, he had himself photographed standing next to the legendary revolutionary. The picture shows a dirty and exhausted man, a stark contrast to the heroic figure he'd once cut; 'Che had a great mane of hair, a look of stern desolation in his face and a dirty beard; his eyes were narrowed with weariness and exhaustion and he had his hands folded, as if they were chained together.'[294]

The army had been anxious to present the murdered guerrilla leader's body in such a way that his identity was clear to everyone; the effect, though, was remarkable; 'the defeated, angry and ragged man of the day before had been transformed into the Christ of Vallegrande, whose clear, open eyes reflected the tender serenity of one who has willingly accepted his sacrifice.'[295]

With this cowardly murder the Bolivian army had solved one problem for itself; but there still remained another, namely what to do with Guevara's body. It did not seem right that the guerrilla leader should be given a 'Christian burial', of the kind that had so magnanimously been granted to Tania; and there was the danger that 'Che's' tomb might become a place of pilgrimage for leftwingers from all over the world. Given its potential for destabilising Bolivia, the authorities wanted to avoid such 'revolutionary tourism' at all costs. The army therefore agreed to have Che's body disappeared. It was clear that they were almost more afraid of the guerrilla leader dead than alive.

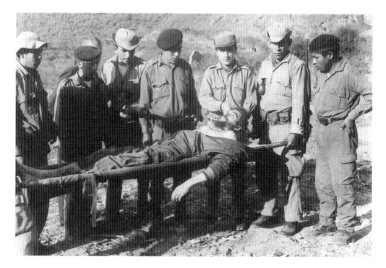

Bolivian soldiers carry the body from the schoolhouse at La Higuera where Che was murdered, 9 October 1967

On the other hand, it was vital that the world, and especially Cuba, be in no doubt of the identity of the body that had been put on display. General Alfredo Ovando Candía suggested cutting off the body's head and preserving the skull as evidence; his colleagues, however, supported a somewhat less barbaric solution. They had Guevara's hands cut off and preserved in formaldehyde. This allowed forensic experts from Buenos Aires to take fingerprints and certify that the hands were indeed Guevara's. Later they found their own tortuous way back to Cuba – three decades before the rest of the revolutionary's mortal remains.

The body could not be burnt; there was no crematorium or oven in which to cremate it. So 'in the dead of night' three soldiers carried out the 'top-secret task' of disposing of Guevara's remains. With them was Captain Vargas Salinas, who in 1995 finally broke the army's stubborn silence and revealed the long-hidden secret. In the early hours of 11 October 1967, members of the army's Pioneer Battalion dug a pit next to the landing strip at the Vallegrande air field; they dumped the bodies of Che and some of his other comrades into it from the back of a lorry, then carefully filled in the grave so that no traces were left behind.

Vargas Salinas' revelation sparked an intensive search for Che's remains. It began with Argentinian experts arriving in the sleepy town of Vallegrande; Cuban scientists from several different fields followed them a short time later and joined the search operation. The operation ended successfully in 1997, when General Hernán Aguilera officially informed Che's brother Roberto that the body of the late Ernesto 'Che' Guevara de la Serna was lying next to the landing strip of the old Vallegrande air field.[296]

At the beginning of July 1997 the press announced 'Guevara's skeleton identified'.[297] Six forensic scientists, three Cubans and three Argentinians, had studied the remains for a week before agreeing

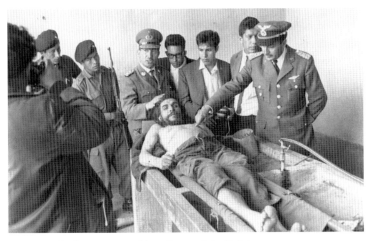

Guevara's body is examined by officers of the Bolivian army

A 'Santera' (an Afro-Cuban priestess who serves a variety of deities) with holy pictures

that they could only belong to Che Guevara. Identification was facilitated by the eleven gunshot wounds that Che had suffered during his life.

Sealed in a coffee-coloured lacquered coffin, Che Guevara left the country he had arrived in 30 years before disguised as the businessman Adolfo Mena González. On 12 July 1997, a Russian Ilyushin jet brought home to Cuba the remains of Che and his Cuban comrades Alberto Fernández Montes de Oca, René Martínez Tamayo, Orlando Pantoja Tamayo and Carlos Coello.

Castro and the entire party and state leadership awaited them at the San Antonio de los Banos military air base. Waiting with them were ranks of uniformed soldiers, who lent a distinctly military atmosphere to the ceremonies. Relatives of the dead man like Che's daughter Aleida Guevara March were lost amid the huge parades that marked the entire day. On 11 October Che's remains were laid at the foot of the statue of José Martí, Cuba's 'national saint', while thousands of Havanans filed past to pay their respects. On 14 October a military cortege carried his remains to Santa Clara, the site of Guevara's greatest triumph, where he won the final decisive victory over Batista's troops. 'Comandante Che Guevara' was laid to rest there on 17 October 1997 in a mausoleum of unrivalled monstrosity, followed by an official ceremony of unrivalled pomposity.[298] During it, his daughter Aleida quoted his words, 'wherever I die is where I want to be.'[299]

Notes

Quotations come from selected works in separate editions, translated and edited by Horst-Eckart Gross.
The following abbreviations are used in the notes:

BOL: *The Complete Bolivian Diaries*, vol. 5, 1992

CUB: *Cuban Diaries*, vol. 2, 1997

GLM: *Guerilla War and Liberation Movements*, vol. 1, 1990

INT: *Writings on Internationalism*, vol. 4, 1997

NM: *The New Man*, vol. 6, 1997

EPOL: *Essays on Economic Policy*, vol. 3, 1995

RCR: *Reminiscences of the Cuban Revolutionary War* 1956–1959, Reinbek 1969

ICGC: *International Che Guevara Conference*, Berlin 1998

1 Quoted in Daniel James, *Che Guevara: Myth and Reality of a Revolutionary*, Munich 1985, p. 35

2 Jon Lee Anderson, *Che: The Biography*, Munich 1997, p. 325

3 Quoted in Michael Lowy, *Che Guevara*, Cologne, 2nd edition 1993, p.13f.

4 Hugo E. Biagini, *Utopias Juveniles: De la bohemia al Che*, Buenos Aires (undated), p.91

5 S. Inti Peredo, *Mi campana con el Che*, La Paz 1970, p.143. In his *Bolivian Diary*, Guevara specifically praised him and his brother with the words *It must be noted that Inti and Coco are emerging ever more clearly as revolutionary and military cadres.* BOL, p.220

6 According to the Cuban politician Armando Hart Davalos in ICGC, p.34

7 Quoted in James, p.34

8 Jorge G. Castaneda, *Companero: the Life and Death of Che Guevara*, London 1997, p.9; also compare with 'le Nouvel Observateur'; 2–8 October 1997, p.4ff.

9 Compare with Biagini, p.101

10 At the same time bringing with it a mass of biographical inconsistencies or plain errors. Examples of this include: 1. His date of birth of 14 June 1928, on which the entire literature is almost unanimous. *Che, A Photographic Album*, p.9, gives it as 14.7.1928. 2. His entry into Havana after the victory of the revolution on 2 January 1959, given in, for example, Volker Skierka, *Fidel Castro* p.93. Variants include Ignacio Taibo II, *Che*, p. 275, where it is given as 3 January 1959. Castro reads out Che's letter of farewell of March 1965 on 3 October 1965; this according to B. May, p. 137. Castaneda p.431 gives it as 5 October 1965. Guevara's death on 9 October 1967; this according to, for example, James, p.517, or Josef Lawrezki, *Ernesto Che Guevara, Life and Struggle of a Revolutionary*, Biography, Frankfurt am Main, 1982, p.462. May, p. 137, gives it as 8 October 1965.

11 Volker Skierka, *Fidel Castro*: A Biography, Berlin 2001, p. 194

12 Anderson, p.405
13 Quoted in ICGC, p.128
14 Ernesto Guevara, *My Son Che*, Hamburg 1986, p.143, 131
15 Ibd., p.131
16 Ibd., p.146
17 Ibd., p.156
18 Ibd., p.178
19 Quoted in May, p.10
20 Guevara, *My Son Che*, p.225
21 Compare with May, p.12
22 Guevara, *My Son Che*, p.233
23 Compare with Anderson, p.28f.
24 Compare for instance with Alicia Dujovne Ortiz, *Evita Peron: The Biography*, Berlin 1996, p.313ff.
25 Compare with Peter Waldmann, 'Argentina' in *Compendium of the History of Latin America*, vol.3, p.889-972, here p.923
26 Compare with James, p.69
27 Ibd., p.72
28 Quoted in May. p.14
29 Quoted in Anderson, p.40
30 Guevara, *My Son Che*, p.256
31 Quoted in Guevara, *My Son Che*, p.277
32 Ibd., p.305
33 Compare with Castaneda, p.52
34 Ibd., p.53f
35 Quoted in May. p.19
36 According to Dolores Moyano, a friend of Che's, in the film *Legends: Che Guevara*, by Andrea Morgenthaler, May 2001.
37 Quoted in Guevara, *My Son Che*, p.322
38 Ibd., p.328
39 Ibd., p.320
40 Compare with Ricardo Rojo, *Che Guevara: Life and Death of a Friend*, Frankfurt am Main 1968, p.20f.
41 Ernesto Che Guevara, *The Motorcycle Diaries*, London 1996, p.20
42 Ibd., p.46, 54
43 Ibd., p.112
44 Ibd., p.131
45 Ibd.
46 Ibd., p.136

47 Alberto Granado, *Travelling with Che Guevara*, London, 2003, p.38
48 Guevara, *Motorcycle Diaries*, p.67
49 Compare with Juana Berges, 'The Latin America young Guevara knew', in *Granma Weekly Review*, October 26, 1975, p.7
50 Granado, p.42
51 Guevara, *Motorcycle Diaries*, p.82
52 Ibd., p.84
53 Granado, p.79
54 Ibd., p.161
55 Guevara, *Motorcycle Diaries*, p.48
56 Ibd., p.19
57 Guevara, *My Son Che*, p.280
58 Compare with ibd., p.399
59 Ibd.
60 Quoted in Anderson, p.47
61 Ernesto Che Guevara, *Otra vez. El diario inedito del segundo viaje por America latina (1953–1956)*, Buenos Aires, 2000.
62 Guevara, My Son Che, p.400ff. It is interesting to note that Guevara Sr. dedicated a second book to his son, entitled *Aqui va un soldado de America*, Buenos Aires, 1987.
63 Compare with Leon E. Bieber, 'Bolivia', in *Compendium of the History of Latin America*, vol.3, p.821-845, here p.833ff.
64 Rojo, p.19
65 Ibd., p.20
66 Ibd.
67 Ibd., p.25f.
68 Ibd.
69 Quoted in Anderson, p.89
70 Maps showing the places they stopped along the journey can be found in Che Guevara, *Otra Vez.*
71 Rojo, p.36
72 Quoted in Anderson, p.98
73 Ernesto Guevara de la Serna to Beatriz Guevara Lynch, 10 December 1953, quoted in Guevara Lynch, *Aqui va*, p.29
74 Compare for example with Mario Lazo Perez, *Recuerdos de la Moncada*, La Habana 1979, who took part in the storming of the barracks.

75 Compare with Niess, *Cuba 20 Times*, p.307ff.

76 Compare with Stephen Schlesinger/Stephen Kinzer, *Banana War: The Case of Guatemala*, Munich 1986, p. 60

77 Compare for example with David Horowitz, *Cold War. Background to US foreign Policy from Yalta to Vietnam*, Berlin 1969, p. 159

78 Compare with Lowy, p.20

79 Compare with May, p.30

80 Quoted in ICGC, p.104

81 Compare with Anderson, p.110

82 Lowy, p.19

83 James, p.125

84 Quoted in Anderson, p.119

85 Compare with ibd., p.115

86 Ibd., p.33

87 From an interview with Lee Lockwood, see Giangiacomo Feltrinelli, ed.: *Latin America – a Second Vietnam?*, Reinbek 1968, p.40f.

88 Rojo, p.62

89 Quoted in Anderson, p.134

90 Compare with Roberto Fernandez Retamar, *Cuba hasta Fidel y para leer al Che*, La Habana 1979, p.51; compare also with Paul Ingenday, 'The Hero without the Cigar. Late Discovery: Che Guevara as Photographer', in *Frankfurter Allgemeine Zeitung*, 4.5.2000, p.44

91 Ernesto Che Guevara, *Venceremos! We Shall Overcome!*, Frankfurt am Main (undated), p.46

92 Quoted in Anderson, p.132

93 'The Influence of the Cuban Revolution on Latin America'. Address to the employees of the Departamento de Seguridad del Estado (18 May 1962) in INT, p.94-122, here p.110f.

94 Compare with Harry Villegas Tamayo, *At the Side of Che Guevara: Interviews with Harry Villegas (Pombo)*, New York 1997, p.16

95 Quoted in Retamar, p.59f.

96 Second Declaration of Havana. Radio Havana Cuba, 4.2.1962, p.28

97 Renee Mendez Capote, *Che, comandante del alba*, La Habana 1998, p.9

98 Quoted in Jose Leopoldo Decamilli, 'Violencia y guerra de guerillas como instrumentos de liberacion en el pensamiento de Ernesto Che Guevara', Berlin 1998, p.8f.

99 Compare with Lowy, p.79

100 CUB, p.10

101 Ernesto Che Guevara, *Reminiscences from the Cuban Revolutionary War 1956–1959*, Reinbek 1969, p.29

102 From a speech given by Fidel Castro in memory of Ernesto Che Guevara in Revolution Square in Havana, 18 October 1967; given in RCR, p.5-16, here p.7

103 Compare with Lowy, p.19

104 Ernesto Guevara de la Serna to Celia Guevara de la Serna, October 1956, quoted in Ernesto Guevara Lynch: *Aqui va un soldado de America*, p.150

105 CUB, p.28

106 Ibd., p.39. A detailed reconstruction based on reports from eyewitnesses and participants can be found in *Granma Weekly Review*, January 23, 1977, p.6f.

107 RCR, p.148

108 CUB, p.90

109 RCR, p.89

110 Ibd., p.138, 140

111 Compare with Pedro Alvarez Tabio/Otto Hernandez, 'An interview that made history', in *Granma Weekly Review*, February 27, 1977

112 *The New York Times*, Sunday, February 24, 1957

113 RCR, p.73

114 Ibd., p.154

115 Compare with Hugh Thomas, *Castro's Cuba*, Berlin 1984, p.124f.

116 Compare with Castro's letter to all anti-Batista groups of 14 December 1957, in RCR, p.163-176

117 CUB, p.282f.
118 Compare with Juergen Hell, *A History of Cuba*, Berlin 1989, p.200
119 CUB, p.285
120 Compare with *Granma Weekly Review*, January 6, 1974; ibd. January 12, 1975, which contains detailed reports on the occasion of 'the 15th Anniversary of the Victory of the Revolution'
121 CUB, p.294f.
122 Compare with May, p.136
123 James, p. 195
124 Compare with Skierka, p.208
125 Anderson, p. 345
126 May, p.53, 55
127 Habel, *Che Guevara*, 1967 – 1997, p.216
128 Taibo II, p.314, 335. 'The roughly 1500 decrees and laws passed in the first year of Castro's Government inaugurated a massive redistribution of wealth.' Alfred Herzka in *Farewell to the Comandante?*, Frankfurt am Main 1998, p.46. Also Fernando Martinez Heredia, 'Cuba: Problemas de la liberacion, la democracia, el socialismo', in *Sintesis* (Madrid), no. 15, September – December 1991, p.181-204, here p.184
129 Quoted in Anderson, p.185
130 Quoted in Anderson, p.331
131 Castaneda, p.178
132 Quoted in Anderson, p.404. A rather crude justification for this associating Guevara with 'war criminals' can be found in Antonio Nunez Jiminez, *On the Road with Fidel*, Berlin 1986, p.53ff.
133 A vehement if not altogether credible accusation of serious human rights abuses against the Cuban regime, and specifically of those committed by Raul Castro, can be found in Armando Valladares, *Against all Hope: Prisoners under Fidel Castro. Memoirs*, Stuttgart, 1988, p.30ff.

134 Skierka, p.211
135 James, p.195
136 Anderson, p.328
137 Compare with *La historia me absolvera*, La Habana 1973
138 Anderson, p.271
139 Compare with Niess, *Cuba 20 Times*, p. 331
140 Skierka, p.157
141 Compare with Anderson, p.41
142 Taibo II, p.384
143 Castaneda, p.216, 221, 223, 220
144 Ibd., p.226
145 Habel, Che Guevara 1967–1997, p.217
146 Compare with Anderson, p.469
147 See 'Tactics and Strategy of the Latin American Revolution (October – November 1962)', in INT, p.138
148 Anderson, p.518f.
149 NM, p.185
150 Ibd., p.15
151 Ibd., p.21
152 Ibd., p.23
153 Ibd., p.53
154 Ibd., p.32
155 Quoted in Roberto Massari, *Che Guevara: Politics and Utopia. The Political and Philosophical Thinking of Ernesto Che Guevara*, Frankfurt am Main 1987, p.163
156 Lowy, p.29f.
157 NM, p.56
158 Ibd., p.20f.
159 Ibd., p.152
160 Ibd., p.144f.
161 Ibd., p.157
162 Ibd., p.160f.
163 Ibd., p.94
164 Ibd., p.140f.
165 Compare with Taibo II, p.307
166 Compare with Anderson, p.276f.
167 Quoted in Anderson, p.367
168 Quoted in Anderson, p.147
169 Quoted in Anderson, p.342f.
170 Ibd., p.358
171 Compare with Castaneda, p.294
172 Quoted in Rojo, p.128
173 Compare with ibd., p.128f.
174 Quoted in Anderson, p.347

175 Compare with Taibo II, p.505
176 Quoted in May, p.87
177 Compare with Frank Niess, *The Colossus of the North*, 2nd ed., Cologne 1986, p.168ff. For the difficulties Washington had in getting the western hemisphere to close ranks against Cuba, see, among other things, 'Time', February 16, 1962, p.34.
178 Anderson, p.438
179 Compare with the 'Department of State Bulletin', February 19, 1962, p.270-284
180 Rojo, p.111
181 Quoted in James, p.224
182 A detailed account of this secret meeting can be found in James, p.224ff.
183 Massari, p.153
184 Compare with James, p.192
185 Massari, p. 195
186 Compare with Massari, p. 157
187 Compare with James, p.198
188 Leo Huberman & Paul M. Sweezy, *Cuba: Anatomy of a Revolution*, Frankfurt am Main 1968, p.224
189 James, p.245
190 Compare with Bettelheim, Castro, Guevara, Mandel, Mora, *Planning, Consciousness and the Law of Value: The Planning Debate in Cuba*, Frankfurt am Main 1969, p.37
191 Ernesto Che Guevara, 'On the Budget Financing System', ibd., p. 47-79, here p.68
192 Compare with Loewy, p.51
193 Quoted in Massari, p. 135
194 Fidel Castro on Che Guevara, 18 October 1967. Voltaire pamphlet 16, Berlin (undated), p.7
195 Quoted in Massari, p.230
196 Compare with Niess, *Sandino: the General of the Oppressed. A Political Biography*, Cologne 1989, passim.
197 GLM, p.133
198 Ibd., p.54
199 Ibd., p.32, 'Cuba – Historical Exception or Vanguard in the Struggle against Imperialism?' (4 April 1961)
200 Ibd.
201 Ibd., p.184
202 GLM, p.62
203 Ibd., p.24
204 Ibd., p.25
205 Quoted in James, p.250
206 Ibd., p.251
207 Castaneda, p.17
208 Ibd., p.351
209 Richard Gott, 'The Last Hours in Dar-es-Salaam: Che Guevara's Guerilla War in Africa. New material on the Cuban Revolution's best-kept secret', *Frankfurter Allgemeine Zeitung*, 18 May 1996
210 Castaneda, p.397
211 For example, the article in 'Granma. Resumen Semanal', 14 de octubre de 1973. Ano 8/Numero 41. Translated in May, *Che Guevara*, p.82ff.
212 INT, p.191f. Cuba – a free country on the American continent. Address to the General Assembly of the United Nations (11 December 1964)
213 Quoted in Anderson, p.538
214 Richard Lege Harris, Death of a Revolutionary: *Che Guevara's Last Mission*, p.75
215 Che Guevara, *The African Dream*, p.23ff.
216 Address at the Second Economic Seminar of Afro-Asian Solidarity, February 1965, in EPOL, p.159-173, here p.162
217 Compare with Castaneda, p.368ff.
218 Compare with Anderson, p.549
219 Maurice Halperin, *The taming of Fidel Castro*, Berkley 1981, p.84
220 Quoted in James, p.285
221 Compare Reynaldo Escobar, 'Congo Mission: A Hymn to Defeat', in *die tageszeitung*, 24 September 1996
222 Compare with Castaneda, p.378
223 Guevara, *The African Dream*, p.27
224 Quoted in Anderson, p.553f.
225 Guevara, *The African Dream*, p.99
226 Ibd., p.48

227 Ibd., p.61
228 Ibd., p.235
229 Compare with 'Frankfurter Allgemeine Zeitung', 18 May 1996
230 Guevara, *The African Dream*, p.248
231 Taibo II, p.491
232 Quoted in Castaneda, p.416
233 Guevara, *The complete Bolivian diaries of Che Guevara and other captured documents*. Ed. by Daniel James. With a new introduction by Henry Butterfield Ryan, New York 2000, p.1
234 Ernesto Sabato in Hector German Oesterheld, Alberto Breccia & Enrique Breccia, *Che, Ernesto Guevara*, Buenos Aires 1997, p.2
235 Compare with James, p.436
236 Quoted in James, p.420
237 Compare with the list of names to be found in The guerilla force during the Bolivian campaign, in Daniel James & Henry Butterfield Ryan (eds.), *The complete Bolivian diaries of Che Guevara*, p.323ff.
238 Ibd., p.74
239 Compare with Jose A. Friedl Zapata, *Tania, the Woman Che Guevara loved*, Berlin 1997, p.7, 19, 27f., 68ff., 100f.
240 Compare with Castaneda, p.433
241 Daniel James & Henry Butterfield Ryan eds., *The complete Bolivian diaries of Che Guevara*, p.ii
242 BOL, p.39
243 Ibd., p.41
244 From the memoirs of the Argentinian painter Ciro Roberto Bustos, who stayed in the guerilla camp from the beginning of March to 20 April 1967; compare with James, p.358f.
245 BOL, p.96, 99
246 Ibd., p.47
247 Compare with Daniel James & Henry Butterfield Ryan eds., *The complete Bolivian diaries of Che Guevara*, p.324ff.

248 Ibd., p.74
249 BOL, p.53
250 Ibd., p.39f.
251 Ibd., p.63
252 Ibd., p.65
253 Ibd., p.81
254 BOL, p.133
256 Compare with Regis Debray, *Revolution within Revolution, Munich* 1967. Extract from it in Feltrinelli ed., *Latin America – a Second Vietnam?* p.165-195
257 Anderson, p.630
258 Ibd., p.631
259 Quoted in May, p.101
260 BOL, p.115
261 Zapata, p.148
262 BOL, p.117
263 Compare with Anderson, p.629, 636
264 BOL, p.139
265 Ibd., p.147
266 Anderson, p.627
267 BOL, p.107
268 Castaneda, p.438
269 James, p.376
270 Compare with Peter Kornbluh, 'The Death of Che Guevara: Declassified', at www.gwu.edu
271 Rius, A-B-Che, p.87
272 BOL, p.135
273 Ibd., p.164, 182, 202, 220
274 Compare with *Granma Weekly Review*, September 5, 1971, and September 11, 1977
275 BOL, p.222
276 Ibd., p.224
277 Ibd., p.218
278 *Der Spiegel*, no.29, 1997, p.122
279 Castaneda, p.58
280 Taibo II, p.493
281 *Stern*, 19.11.1967
282 BOL, p.202, 220
283 Castaneda, p.577
284 Taibo II, p.581
285 Castaneda, p.498
286 Taibo II, p.586
287 Heinz Dieterich Steffan in ICGC, p.133f.
288 Ibd., p.41f.

289 Peter Kornbluh, 'The Death of Che Guevara: Declassified', at www.gwu.edu

290 Castaneda, p.499

291 Anderson, p.664

292 Compare, among other things, with 'Interpress Politics', International Biographical Press Service, No.62/92, May 1968, p.2. Several other sources give 8 October 1967 as the day of his death. Compare with Suarez Salazar, Futuridad del Che, p.15, who in as well as this still claims that Che was killed 'in battle'.

293 Taibo II, p.592

294 Ibd., p.587

295 Castaneda, p.9

296 *Der Spiegel*, 27/1997, p.131

297 For example, 'Frankfurter Rundschau', 7 July 1997

298 For this see *Tu eterna presencia: tributo al Che y sus companeros de la gesta boliviana 1997*. La Habana 1997, passim

299 According to AFP, 6 July 1997

Chronology

Year	Date	Life
1927	10 November	Ernesto Guevara Lynch and Celia de la Serna marry in Buenos Aires.
1928	14 June	Ernesto Guevara de la Serna born in Rosario, Argentina.
1930		Ernesto suffers his first asthma attack.
1932		The doctors advise a change of climate. The family moves to Alta Gracia, not far from Cordoba.
1937		Ernesto Guevara Senior founds a Committee for the Defence of the Spanish Republic in Alta Gracia.
1941		He enters the *Colegio Nacional Dean Funes* in Córdoba.

Year	History	Culture
1927	Josef Stalin comes to power in the USSR. Charles Lindbergh flies across the Atlantic.	BBC public radio launched. Virginia Woolf, *To the Lighthouse.*
1928	Kellogg-Briand Pact for Peace. Alexander Fleming discovers penicillin.	Maurice Ravel, *Bolero.* D H Lawrence, *Lady Chatterley's Lover.* W B Yeats, *The Tower.*
1930	Mahatma Gandhi leads Salt March in India. Frank Whittle patents turbo-jet engine. Planet Pluto discovered.	The Hays Office introduces the Production Code guidelines of moral standards in the US cinema.
1932	First autobahn opened between Cologne and Bonn.	Aldous Huxley, *Brave New World.* Bertholt Brecht, *The Mother.*
1937	Japan invases China: Nanjing massacre. Arab-Jewish conflict in Palestine.	Jean-Paul Sartre, *La Nausée.* John Steinbeck, *Of Mice and Men.* Picasso, *Guernica.*
1941	Operation Barbarossa: Germany invades the Soviet union. Italians expelled from Somalia, Ethiopia and Eritrea. In US, Lend-Lease Bill passed. Churchill and F D Roosevelt sign the Atlantic Charter. Japan attacks Pearl Harbour.	Orson Welles, *Citizen Kane.* Bertholt Brecht, *Mother Courage and her Children.*

Year	Date	Life
1946	24 February	Juan Domingo Perón is elected constitutional President of Argentina.
1947	November	Ernesto begins studying medicine at the University of Buenos Aires.
1950	1 January	He sets off on his first journey to northern Argentina.
1952	4 January	With his friend Alberto Granado he begins his first journey across South America, visiting Chile, Peru, the Amazon, Columbia and Venezuela. He returns via Miami in October 1952.

Year	History	Culture
1946	Juan Peron becomes president of Argentina. National Health Service founded in Britain. Winston Churchill makes 'Iron Curtain' speech in Fulton.	Bertrand Russell, *History of Western Philosophy*. Jean Paul Sartre, *Being and Nothingness*. Jean Cocteau, *La Belle et la Bête*.
1947	Truman Doctrine: US promises economic and military aid to countries threatened by Soviet expansion plans. India becomes independent. Chuck Yeager breaks the sound barrier.	Tennessee Williams, *A Streetcar Named Desire*.
1950	Schuman Plan. Korean War begins. China invades Tibet.	Eugene Ionescu, *The Bald Prima Donna*. Billy Wilder, *Sunset Boulevard*.
1952	Gamal Abdel Nasser leads coup in Egypt. European Coal and Steel community formed; Britain refuses to join. US tests hydrogen bomb. Elizabeth II becomes queen of Britain.	Samuel Beckett, *Waiting for Godot*. Hemingway, *The Old Man and the Sea*. Steinbeck, *East of Eden*. Gary Cooper and Grace Kelly in *High Noon*.

Year	Date	Life
1953	January	His engagement with Chichina Ferreyra is broken off.
	March	He graduates as Doctor of Medicine from the University of Buenos Aires.
	July	He begins his second journey across Latin America, this time with his friend Carlos Ferrer; after a long stay in Bolivia he visits Peru, Ecuador, Costa Rica and Guatemala.
	End of 1953	First contact with Cuban revolutionaries in San Jose, Costa Rica.
1954	January	Meets Hilda Gadea Acosta in Guatemala. Turns towards Marxism; the revolutionary 'Che' Guevara is born.
	27 June	Jacobo Arbenz, Guatemala's reforming president, is forced to resign.
	3 July	'Operation Success', a US intervention against Arbenz, is crowned with success: Washington's puppet Castillo Armas takes over power. Ernesto flees to Mexico.
	21 September	Arrival in Mexico.
	24 September	In a letter to his mother Che mentions in passing his marriage to Hilda Gadea.
1955	15 February	birth of their daughter Hilda Beatriz, known as Hildita.
	July/August	Ernesto Guevara is introduced to Fidel Castro. After a discussion lasting into the early hours of the morning, Castro persuades Guevara to become a doctor on his expedition to liberate Cuba from the dictator Bastita.

Year	History	Culture
1953	Eisenhower becomes US president. Stalin dies. Korean War ends. Francis Crick and James Watson discover double helix (DNA).	Dylan Thomas, *Under Milk Wood*.
1954	Insurrection in Algeria. French defeat at Dien Bien Phu and withdrawal from Indochina: Ho Chi Minh forms government in North Vietnam.	Bill Haley and the Comets, 'Rock around the Clock.' *On the Waterfront*, with Marlon Brando.
1955	West Germany joins NATO. Warsaw Pact formed.	Vladimir Nabokov, *Lolita*. Tolkien, *The Lord of the Rings*. Waugh, *Officers and Gentlemen*.

Year	Date	Life
1956	25 November	The *Granma* leaves the Mexican port of Tuxpan for Cuba, with Che and the Cuban rebels on board.
	2 December	The rebels land on the south west coast of Cuba.
	5 December	A surprise attack by the army causes heavy losses.
1957	17 January	The rebels attack a garrison at the mouth of the La Plata river, winning their first victory.
	17 February	Castro is interviewed by the American journalist Herbert L. Matthews.
		Throughout the year: skirmishes with Batista's troops in the Sierra Maestra; Guevara is appointed '*Comandante*'.
1958	9 April	General Strike fails.
	25 May	Batista's troops launch a counter-offensive.
	31 December	Guevara wins the decisive battle against Batista's troops in the provincial capital of Santa Clara.
1959	1 January	Batista flees abroad.
	2 January	Guevara and Camilo Cienfuegos make a triumphal entry into Havana.
	9 February	Che is made a 'native' Cuban citizen.
	3 June	Marriage to Aleida March de la Forre.
	13 June–8 September	Goodwill journey to African and Asian states as well as to Yugoslavia.
	7 October	Appointed head of the industry department of the INRA (National Institute of Agrarian Reform).
	7 October	President of the National Bank.

Year	History	Culture
1956	Nikita Khrushchev denounces Stalin. Suez Crisis. Revolts in Poland and Hungary. Transatlantic telephone service links the US to the UK.	Lerner (lyrics) and Loewe (music), *My Fair Lady*. Elvis Presley, 'Heartbreak Hotel,' 'Hound Dog,' 'Love me Tender.' John Osborne, *Look Back in Anger*.
1957	Treaty of Rome: EEC formed. USSR launches Sputnik 1. The Gold Coast becomes independent Ghana.	The Academy excludes anyone on the Hollywood blacklist from consideration for Oscars.
1958	Fifth French Republic; Charles de Gaulle becomes president. Great Leap Forward launched in China.	Boris Pasternak, *Dr Zhivago*. Claude Lévi-Strauss, *Structural Anthropology*. Harold Pinter, *The Birthday Party*.
1959	In the US, Alaska and Hawaii are admitted to the Union. Solomon Bandaranaike, PM of Ceylon is assassinated.	Buddy Holly dies in a plane crash. *Ben Hur* (dir. William Wyler). Gunter Grass, *The Tin Drum*.

Year	Date	Life
1960	24 July October/ December	Signs a trade agreement between Cuba and China. Head of an economic delegation visiting Czechoslovakia, the Soviet Union, China, North Korea, East Germany and Hungary. Trade and credit agreements signed with these countries.
1961	23 February Mid-April 6-17 August 8 and 16 August 18 August 19 August	Guevara is appointed Minister for Industry. Bay of Pigs invasion. Inter-American Economic Council holds its conference in Punta del Este, Uruguay. Guevara delivers speeches at this conference. Meets the Argentinian President Arturo Frondizi in Buenos Aires. Meets the Brazilian President Janio da Silva Quadros in Brasilia.
1962	31 January 3 February October	Cuba expelled from the Organisation of American States (OAS). US President John F. Kennedy announces a trade embargo against Cuba. Missile Crisis.
1963	2 July July	Visit to Prague. Journey through Algeria.

Year	History	Culture
1960	Vietnam War begins. OPEC formed. Oral contraceptives marketed.	Federico Fellini, *Dolce Vita*. Alfred Hitchcock, *Psycho*.
1961	Berlin Wall erected. Yuri Gagarin is the first man in space. U2 Affair.	The Rolling Stones are formed. Rudolf Nureyev defects from the USSR.
1962	Cuban Misile Crisis. Jamaica, Trinidad and Tobago, and Uganda become independent.	Edward Albee, *Who's Afraid of Virginia Woolf?* David Lean, *Lawrence of Arabia*.
1963	J F Kennedy assassinated; Martin Luther King leads March on Washington. Kenya becomes independent. Organisation of African Unity formed.	Betty Friedan, *The Feminine Mystique*. The Beatles, 'She Loves You.' Luchino Visconti, *The Leopard*.

Year	Date	Life
1964	25 March	Speech before the World Trade Conference (UNCTAD) in Geneva.
	4 November	Heads of a Cuban delegation to celebrate the 47th Anniversary of the October Revolution in Moscow.
	10-12 December	Attends the General Assembly of the UN in New York, where he delivers a speech.
1965	19 December 1964-13 March 1965	Visits eight African states; attempts to set up a 'common front against colonialism, imperialism and neo-colonialism'.
	25 February	Attends an economic seminar at the Afro-Asian Solidarity Conference in Algiers and delivers a speech strongly criticising the Soviet Union.
	14 March	Returns to Havana; conflict with Castro; retires from all public offices and renounces his Cuban citizenship. He disappears for months from public view.
	19 April	In Dar-es-Salaam, Tanzania.
	3 October	Castro makes public Guevara's letter of farewell, written in March.
	22 November	Guevara and his men leave the Congo after the failure of the guerilla war.

Year	History	Culture
1964	Kruschev ousted by Leonid Brezhnev. First race relations act in Britain. Civil Rights act in US. PLO is formed.	Harnick (lyrics) and Bock (music) *Fiddler on the Roof*. Saul Bellow, *Herzog*. Stanley Kubrick, *Doctor Strangelove*.
1965	Military coup in Indonesia. Unilateral declaration of independence in Rhodesia.	Neil Simon, *The Odd Couple*.

Year	Date	Life
1966	March	Returns from Africa.
	July	Begins preparations for the Bolivian operation.
	October	Travels to Bolivia by a circuitous route.
	3 November	Arrival in Bolivia under the name of Adolfo Mena Gonzalez.
	7 November	Arrival at the guerilla camp in Nancahuazu; first diary entry.
	31 December	A meeting with Mario Monje, the head of the Bolivian Communist Party, fails to produce an agreement; Tania arrives in the camp.
1967	23 March	The guerillas clash prematurely with Bolivian soldiers. From then on the army is on their trail.
	May onwards	End of contact with La Paz and Havana.
	14 August	Government troops find documents belonging to the guerillas.
	30 August	Part of Che's group is destroyed; death of Tania.
	7 October	Last diary entry.
	8 October	The guerillas are ambushed in the Quebrada del Yuro gorge; Che is wounded, captured and taken to La Higuera.
	9 October, 1.10pm	Ernesto Che Guevara is executed. His body is taken to Vallegrande, put on show and then secretly disposed of.
1997	July	Guevara's body is exhumed from the Vallegrande air field.
	12 July	Che's mortal remains are transported to Cuba.
	17 October	After an official ceremony with full military honours, Che's remains are interred in a specially constructed mausoleum in Santa Clara.

Year	History	Culture
1966	France withdraws its troops from NATO. In the US race riots.	John Lennon speculates that The Beatles are more popular than Jesus. The Band gives their last concert.
1967	Six Day War in the Middle East. First heart transplant performed in Cape Town.	The Beatles, *Sergeant Pepper's Lonely Hearts Club Band*. Gabriel García Márquez, *One Hundred Years of Solitude*. Tom Stoppard, *Rosencrantz and Guildenstern are Dead*.
1997	Deng Xiao-ping dies. The British colony of Hong Kong reverts to Chinese control. Diana Princess of Wales, is killed in a car crash in Paris.	Frank Gehry, *Guggenheim Museum* in Bilbao. Nobel Prize for Literature awarded to Dario Fo. IBM computer Deep Blue defeats world chess champion Garry Kasparov.

Testimonies

Fidel Castro

If we wanted to describe a person who belonged not to our own time but rather to the future, then I declare with all my heart that Che would be such a person, a man without a stain, without a single stain on his conduct. And if we wanted to describe how we would like our children to be, then we, as passionate revolutionaries, would fervently cry, Let them be like Che!

> 18 October 1967 (Jon Lee Anderson,
> *Che: The Biography*, 1997)

Jean-Paul Sartre

I believe that this man was not only an intellectual, but the most perfect man of his time.

> (Daniel James, *Che Guevara*, 1997)

Janette Habel

Che was the embodiment of an ethical conception of power, a political leader of a new type, who made his deeds correspond to his words.

> (Albert Sterr, *The Left in Latin America*, 1997)

Raul Roa

His image was imprinted on my memory: sparkling intelligence, ascetic pallor, asthmatic breathing, high forehead, thick hair, dry manner, strong chin, relaxed bearing, penetrating glance, acute mind, quiet voice, vibrant sensuality, clear laugh, and a cloud of magical dreams surrounded his figure.

(Paco Ignacio Taibo II, Che: The Biography
of Ernesto Che Guevara, 1997)

Ernesto Sabato

Ernesto Guevara did not die merely to raise living standards in the poorest parts of the world. For me, and, I believe, for many others, in fact for millions of people and above all for those who mourned his death, he died for an ideal that is infinitely more precious; the ideal of a new human being.

(Hector German Oesterheld, *Che: Ernesto Guevara/dibujos*, 1997)

Ernesto Kroch

Che Guevara was a fascinating individual. For the young he was and is more than that – he is an idol. The fascination he exerts probably has less to do with his political and economic ideas and much more with how he lived and what he did. At some point, most revolutionaries turn into more or less normal politicians. By contrast, Che embodies to some extent a person of commitment, one who constantly and persistently champions his ideals [...].

('ila. Journal of the Latin American Information Bureau', 1997)

Daniel James

If we consider Che from a historical perspective and impartially compare him on the one hand to Fidel, and on the other to Mao or Ho or Giap, then we begin to see how overrated his reputation has become, and how much more myth it contains than reality. Of course, his personality contributed a great deal to that myth: he was daring, brave, honest, irreverent, uncompromising, a fighter through and through, as he proved time and time again.

(Daniel James, Che Guevara. Myth and
Truth of a Revolutionary, 1997)

Picture Sources

The author and publishers wish to express their thanks to the following sources of illustrative material and/or permission to reproduce it. They will make the proper acknowledgements in future editions in the even that any ommissions have occurred.

Freddy Alborta: pp. 134,135; *Bohemia*: p. 76; Casa de las Américas: pp. i, 111; Raul Corrales: p. 35; dpa Archive, Hamburg: pp. 28, 80; Ediciones Verde Olivo: pp 78, 106; Elmar May, *Che Guevara*, Reinbek, 1973: p. 124; Luis Favre: p. 57; Funcadión de la Natureleza y El Hombre: p.38; Robert van der Hilst: p. 136; Keystone Pictures: p. 12; Eduardo Longoni, Buenos Aires: p. 25; Guevara Lynch Archive: pp.5, 6, 9, 16, 19, 36; Frank Niess Collection: p. 87 (Photo: Angelika Kuritka); Liberio Noval: pp. 58, 101, 103; Oficina de Asuntos Historicós, Havana: pp. 46, 48, 55, 62, 69; Prensa Latina: pp. 64, 66, 100, 130; Susanne Rescio: pp. ii, 1; Perfecto Romero: p. 62; Andrew St George: p 52; Saucedo Archive: p. 125; *Traum des Rebellen*, García, Sola, Rütten & Loening, Berlin, 1997: pp. 7, 71, 114, 117.

Index

About the Author

Frank Niess, born in 1942 in Blankenfelde near Berlin, studied German literature, history and political science at the universities of Bonn and Heidelberg. He took his doctorate in 1972 and became a member of the editorial staff of Sudwestrundfunk. He lives in Heidelberg. Other publications include *The Colossus of the North: History of Latin American policy in the USA*; reprinted 1986. *The Heritage of the Conquista: A History of Nicaragua, reprinted 1989, Sandino: The General of the Oppressed. A Political Biography*, 1989. *Cuba Twenty Times*, 1991. *In the Beginning was Columbus: A History of Underdevelopment. Latin America from 1492 to the Present*, reprinted 1992. *One World or No World. From Nationalism to Global Politics*, 1994. *The European Idea. From the Spirit of Resistance*, reprinted 2002.